TO: ━━━━━━━━━━━━━━━━━━━━

FROM: ━━━━━━━━━━━━━━━━━━━━

What are folks saying about the Simplified Cowboy Version?

"It is truly a blessing to have the Simplified Cowboy Version. Now reading the Lord's Good Book doesn't leave me feelin' like a cow looking at a new gate!!"
–Richard Thompson, Stanton, TX

"This is truly a 'No nonsense, no dog and pony show, no snake-oil, real cowboy's way of understanding a real God's words' ".
–Pastor Frank Johnson, Cow Camp Cowboy Church, Weatherford TX

"Kevin Weatherby's work has made a world of difference in my life and his interpretations through the Simplified Cowboy Version give it to you straight."
–Trey Wahrmund

"When a cowboy or cowgirl picks up God's word, they should be able to understand what God is telling them! SCV has done that with a flair that is permeated in the Western heritage language, something all can understand: man, woman or child. God Bless Kevin Weatherby and his work!"
–Pastor Kevin Mahr, Cowboy Church of Lee County, Lexington TX

"Kevin Weatherby and Save the Cowboy understand the importance of reaching men where they are. By integrating the cowboy lifestyle and language, SCV has successfully made Scripture relevant to a new generation of outlaws in need of a Trail Boss."
–Evan Dawson, founder of Third Option Men

"The Simplified Cowboy Version is as simple as that, simple and cowboy. I've been reaching out to cowboys for years, at rodeo bible camps and other events. The number one thing I hear is "The Bible doesn't make sense and it's hard to read." I believe the SCV will help open their eyes and lead more cowboys to the greener pastures."
–Pastor Walter Taylor, Catalyst Cowboy Church, Endicott WA

"Call it a cowboy concordance. It's not meant to replace the Bible, but does make it a whole lot easier to understand."
–Cory Johnson, Waller TX

"Thank you for the SCV. It brings things to light in a language that is easier to relate to and understand."
–Kim Casey, Elbert County CO

"What a ministry! The SCV is doing what a modern day Paul would do—figure out a person's culture, and then go to them and tell them about Christ in a way that they can understand. Here it is COWBOY!"
–Pastor Josh Sparkman, No Fences Cowboy Church, Falkville AL

The Simplified Cowboy Version is not a Bible. It is a Bible paraphrase intended to help those that are new to the Word of God and also those that want to see the Bible come alive in a brand new way. This undertaking wasn't done by scholars or theologians, just two cowboys who have a love for the Bible and helpin' cowboys and cowgirls understand its vast beauty. The scripture references are there so you can go get a real Bible and see what God really has to say.

We'll see ya down the trail, amigos!

Kevin Weatherby

Jake Hershey

Matthew 1

The Family Tree

This is a list of how Jesus came all the way from Abraham and down through King David (because it was said long ago that God's Boy would come through David):

² Abraham was Isaac's daddy.
 Isaac was Jacob's daddy.
 Jacob was Judah and his brothers' daddy.
³ Judah was Perez and Zerah's daddy (Tamar was their momma).
 Perez was Hezron's daddy.
 Hezron was Ram's daddy.
⁴ Ram was Amminadab's daddy.
 Amminadab was Nahshon's daddy.
 Nahshon was Salmon's daddy.
⁵ Salmon was Boaz' daddy (Rahab was his momma).
 Boaz was Obed's daddy (Ruth was his momma).
 Obed was Jesse's daddy.
⁶ Jesse was King David's daddy.
 David was Solomon's daddy (whose momma was Bathsheba, the widow lady of Uriah).
⁷ Solomon was Rehoboam's daddy.
 Rehoboam was Abijah's daddy.
 Abijah was Asa's daddy.
⁸ Asa was Jehoshaphat's daddy.
 Jehoshaphat was Jehoram's daddy.
 Jehoram was Uzziah's daddy.
⁹ Uzziah was Jotham's daddy.
 Jotham was Ahaz' daddy.
 Ahaz was Hezekiah's daddy.
¹⁰ Hezekiah was Manasseh's daddy.
 Manasseh was Amon's daddy.
 Amon was Josiah's daddy.
¹¹ Josiah was Jehoiachin and his brothers' daddy.

In verses 1-17, God worked through all sorts of different people to bring Jesus into the world—David was a king, Rahab was a hooker, Ram was just a regular guy. Given that God used a king, a hooker and a regular guy, do you think he could use you?

¹² After the Babylonian boot out:
Jehoiachin was Shealtiel's daddy.
Shealtiel was Zerubbabel's daddy.
¹³ Zerubbabel was Abiud's daddy.
Abiud was Eliakim's daddy.
Eliakim was Azor's daddy.
¹⁴ Azor was Zadok's daddy.
Zadok was Akim's daddy.
Akim was Eliud's daddy.
¹⁵ Eliud was Eleazar's daddy.
Eleazar was Matthan's daddy.
Matthan was Jacob's daddy.
¹⁶ Jacob was Joseph's daddy, and Joseph was hitched to Mary.
Mary gave birth to Jesus, who is called the Saving Hero.

¹⁷ So there were fourteen generations from Abraham until David. Then there was another fourteen from David till the time the Jews were taken captive to Babylon, and fourteen from the captivity in Babylon until the Christ.

Joseph and the Birth of Jesus

¹⁸ Before Jesus was born, Joseph had asked for Mary's hand in marriage. Joseph had been honorable towards Mary and she was unspoiled. But before they could get hitched, Mary became pregnant through the power of the Holy Ghost. ¹⁹ In order to avoid an embarrassing shotgun wedding, Joseph was just gonna go away and leave Mary quietly.

²⁰ While Joseph sat ponderin' his options, an angel appeared to him and told him not to run out on Mary. Seems her baby wasn't by any human, but conceived by the Holy Ghost. ²¹ "She's gonna have a son," the angel said. "Be sure and call him Jesus, 'cause he's gonna end up savin' everyone from their sins."

²² This all happened because a prophet had already said, ²³ "A gal that's never been with a man will have her a child and call him Emmanuel." — which is a fancy way of sayin', "God's with us."

²⁴ Joseph went and did just what that angel told him to and tied the knot with Mary. ²⁵ But he didn't never go to her bed like a husband would usually do until after Jesus was born.

In verse 18, even though Joseph found out that Mary was in a family way before they were married, he refused to shun her in public. When you find out about someone's "dirty laundry," do you say a prayer for them or do you talk about it at the cow sale?

In verses 20-24, while gettin' hitched to a pregnant gal could have made him look like a fool, Joseph did what God wanted him to do. Have you done what God wants you to do, even when other people thought it was crazy?

Matthew 2

Strangers from Afar

After Jesus was born in Bethlehem, while Herod was King, some strangers from the east visited Jerusalem [2] and asked, "Where's the little one that's meant to be the King of the Jews? We seen a bright light from way over yonder and we have come to hit a knee before him."

[3] King Herod was plum disturbed along with all of Jerusalem at the things the strangers said. [4] He gathered up every person that worked around there that had a lick of sense and asked 'em where the Christ was to be born. [5] They all told him it was supposed to be in Bethlehem based on what a wise fellow of God had said:

> [6] *"Bethlehem ain't no little place among Judah. From you will come a cowboy that will gather all of the herd together and take care of 'em."*

[7] Then Herod asked those strangers when the bright light had appeared in the sky. [8] He told 'em to ride for Bethlehem and find this baby they was a lookin' for and send him a message. Herod wanted to come and grab a knee with his hat in his hands right along with them.

[9] The strangers rode hard and followed the light until it stopped over where Jesus was layin'. [10] When they saw the bright star, they was overcome with happiness. [11] When they got to the house and saw Mary holdin' Jesus, they grabbed a knee and worshiped him. Then they went to their saddlebags and brought out some sure enough nice gifts for the baby. [12] They rode off at first light, but they didn't return to old Herod. An angel had told them to take another trail and strike a long trot back to where they'd come from.

The Getaway

[13] After the strangers had lit out, an angel came to Joseph while he was dreamin'. "Saddle up," the angel told him, "ride hard for Egypt and hunker down there until I tell you it's safe. Herod's gonna start killin' all the kids and he's hopin' Jesus is one of 'em."

In verses 1-2, the three wise men (strangers) came looking for Jesus with gifts to give him, rather than expecting Jesus to give something to them. Do you come to Jesus asking what he can do for you—or what you can do for him?

In verse 11, the wise men (strangers) gave Jesus gold, incense and spice, which were the best things they had to offer. When you give things to Christ—your attention, your time, your efforts—is it the best you have to offer?

[14] So Joseph took Mary and Jesus and struck a long lope for Egypt. [15] He stayed there until Herod had kicked the bucket. This fulfilled a long ago sayin' that said: "My Son's gonna come out of Egypt when I call for him."

[16] When old Herod realized he'd been double crossed by the strangers, he was spittin' nails. He gave orders to slaughter all the boys in the territory that were two years old or younger. That's the age the strangers had reckoned Jesus to be. [17] This also brought truth to a long ago foretelling by the prophet Jeremiah:

> [18] *"There will be wailin' and weepin'. Rachel will cry for her kids and won't take to any comfortin' by anyone because they are all gone."*

Headin' Home

[19] When Herod was dead, an angel once again came to Joseph in a dream and [20] told him, "Light out for home. Take Jesus and his momma back. The danger has passed on by."

[21] So Joseph saddled up and they traveled back to Israel. [22] But when he found out that Archelaus had taken his father Herod's place on the throne, he became scared. Another dream had warned him, so he detoured into Galilee territory, [23] and made permanent camp in a place called Nazareth. Once again, this made true the old saying: "He's gonna be called a Nazarene."

Matthew 3

John the Baptist Blazes a Trail for Jesus

Durin' this time, John the Baptist was preachin' in the dry country of Judea [2] and tellin' folks, "Make right your minds, for God's Green Pasture is near." [3] John is who Isaiah was talkin' about when he said:

> *"The dry country will have a voice, 'Blaze a trail for the Lord and make it true and straight.'"*

[4] John's duds were made out of animal hair, and his belt was made of good leather. He made meals out of locusts with wild honey for dessert. [5] Cowboys and cowgirls

---

In verse 16, King Herod was afraid Jesus would take over and run his outfit—when Jesus really came to give him eternal life, something worth much more than what Herod had. Do you know cowboys who are afraid that ridin' for Jesus will mean giving up something they think is "valuable"?

In verses 1-2, John the Baptist told people to turn to God so God would forgive their sins—which meant John was inviting sinful, messed-up, dirty outlaws to meet God. Have you ever thought you had to get spit-shined before you could meet God?

came from all over to see him. [6] These cowboys and cowgirls told God about everything they'd done wrong and John baptized them in Jordan Creek.

[7] When John saw the real religious folks ride over the hill followed by a bunch of no-account politicians, he hollered at them: "You den of rattlesnakes!! Who told you to ride as fast as you could from the comin' anger? [8] You gotta change the way you live your life if you want what God is offerin' folks here! [9] Don't even try to make the excuse that Abraham was your father. God can make these rocks become Abraham's children if that's what he wants to do. It don't mean nothin'. [10] God's axe is already at the bottom of your tree. If you don't change the way you live your lives, your tree will end up in the BBQ pit.

[11] "I dunk folks in water as a symbol that they want to change the way they think and live. But there's a cowboy comin' who's boots I ain't fit for carrying. He's gonna dunk you with the Holy Ghost and flame. [12] His pitchfork is in his hand and he's gonna separate the good stuff from the moldy. This useless trash will be thrown in the fire that can't go out."

[13] Then Jesus rode in from Galilee to be dunked in the Jordan by John. [14] Old John balked at the idea and said, "It's the other way around! I need to be dunked by you."

[15] But Jesus told him, "Nope. This is the way we're gonna do it so everything will be made right with God." John shook his head in disbelief but agreed to do it Jesus' way.

[16] As soon as Jesus had come up out of the creek, heaven's gate was throwed wide open. The Spirit of God came out of that gate in the form of a dove and landed on Jesus. [17] Out of heaven a voice said, "This is my Son that I love. I am pleased with everything that he is."

Matthew 4

The Duel in the Desert

God led Jesus out into the dry country to be tempted by the devil. [2] Jesus was famished after not eating for forty days and nights. [3] That old devil rode up and said, "If you're God's Boy, you can easily turn these rocks into bread. What are you waitin' on?"

In verse 8, John told people to not only talk the talk, but walk the walk—meaning they should not just say good things but actually do good things. Have you known people who only say the right things, but don't do the right things?

In verse 13, Jesus was baptized, even though he never sinned, as an example for the rest of us to be baptized. Have you known people who said they followed God but thought they didn't need to be dunked?

[4] Jesus said, "Man don't live on just bread, but on every word that comes out of God's mouth."

[5] The devil snatched Jesus up and took him to the holy city and they stood at the highest point of the church. [6] "If you're God's Boy," the devil said, "bail off of here. 'Cause it's written that:

> *"God's angels are gonna look out for you. They won't let a scratch of harm come to you."*

[7] Jesus answered and said, "It's also said: 'Don't be a fool and try to test God.'"

[8] The devil whisked him off again and took him to a tall mountain where they could see all of the territories. [9] "I'll make a horse trade with you. I'll swap you everything you see below us if you'll take off your hat and call me boss."

[10] Jesus told him, "Get away from me Satan! It's written that we are to 'Only bow down and call God the boss; him and him only.'"

[11] The devil then high-tailed it out of there and God sent some angels to take care of his Boy.

Jesus Starts Tellin' Folks the Truth

[12] Jesus heard that his buddy John the Baptist had been thrown in jail so he rode back to Galilee. [13] When he left Nazareth, he bunked out in Capernaum [14] to prove what was once said by Isaiah:

> [15] *"In the land around Capernaum and along the Jordan, and in Galilee, the land of those who ain't Jews, [16] the folks livin' in the dark have seen a bright light; those livin' in the land shadowed by death, a great lantern has been lit in the darkness."*

[17] From the first time Jesus told folks the truth, he said, "Change the way you think and live, for God's Green Pastures are close."

Some Cowboys Decide to Ride with Jesus

[18] When Jesus was walkin' down by the Sea of Galilee, he saw two cowboys, Peter and his brother Andrew. They were gatherin' some cattle and puttin' 'em in some pens. [19] "Come and ride with me," Jesus said to 'em, "and help me gather mavericks. I'll make

---

In verses 2-11, Satan tempted Jesus to stop Him from doin' what he'd come to do, which was to show cowboys the trail that led into the kingdom of heaven (not a kingdom on earth). Do you think Satan has tempted you to stop you from God's purpose for your life?

Also in verses 2-11, Satan tempted Jesus when he was plum give out—when Jesus was alone, hungry and tired during his time in the desert. The next time you are feeling weaker than a newborn calf, will you watch out for Satan to tempt you?

you gatherers of men." [20] They left the herd right there and rode off with him.

[21] As they rode along, Jesus saw two more cowboys—James and his brother John. They were also getting' ready to work some cattle. Jesus hollered at them to come on [22] and they immediately dropped what they were doin' and rode off with him.

[23] Jesus traveled everywhere in Galilee. He was teachin', preachin', and healin' all kinds of folks. [24] Word traveled near and far about what he was doin'. People came from everywhere so Jesus could help them. [25] Huge herds of mavericks, from Galilee to the area on the other side of Jordan Creek, began to follow him.

Matthew 5

The Message on the Mesa

When Jesus saw the great big herd of mavericks, he rode up on a mesa and hunkered down there. His cowboys grabbed a knee right below him, [2] and he began to tell them:

[3] "God takes mighty good care of those folks that don't have anything to depend on except him.

[4] "God takes mighty good care of those folks who are hurtin' and sad because he's the only one that can offer 'em comfort.

[5] "God takes mighty good care of those that don't think very highly of themselves and he's gonna give 'em everything one day.

[6] "God takes mighty good care of those that would rather do what he says than eat or drink, for one day they will never be hungry or thirsty again.

[7] "God takes mighty good care of those that don't have an ounce of cruelty in 'em, for one day they will be spared.

[8] "God takes mighty good care of those whose hearts are as pure as spring water, 'cause they will sure enough see God one day.

[9] "God takes mighty good care of those who don't make trouble for anyone, for he's gonna claim them as his own sons.

Also in verses 2-11 (back on page 6), Satan tempted Jesus through his strengths, because Jesus had the power to satisfy his needs anyway he wanted to, even the wrong way—but he didn't. Since Jesus was tempted the same ways you are tempted, don't you think he can help you resist those tempting things too?

In verses 18-22 (back on page 6), when Jesus called the disciples to follow him, they did not make excuses, because they knew Jesus could change their lives for the better. When you feel like Jesus is calling you to ride for him, do you make excuses or do you follow him to a better life?

[10] God takes mighty good care of those who are put-down because of their belief in him and the way they live, for their reward is his green, eternal pasture.

[11] "God's gonna take real special care of those of you who are insulted, spit upon, and talked wrongly about because of me. [12] Just smile and go on because your reward will be more than worth it in heaven. They did the same things to the cowboys that worked for God so many years ago.

Salt and Light

[13] "Ya'll are the salt of the earth. If the seasoning loses its flavor, how can it be seasoned again? It ain't good for anything anymore, so it will be thrown out in the backyard to be trampled on by boots and coyotes.

[14] "Ya'll are the light of this earth. You can't miss a big city that sits on a hill. [15] And cowboys don't light a lantern and then throw their hat on top of it to keep it from shinin'. [16] Just like that, let your lanterns shine bright before men, so that they can see all the good things you do and bow their heads in thanks to the Boss.

Jesus Gives It to 'Em Straight

[17] "Don't think that I've come here to take away any of the things the Boss told you to do. I didn't come to take anything away, but to show you the right trail. [18] I ain't lyin' when I say that nothing will be changed in what he told you to do until everything is finished. [19] Any cowboy that doesn't do what the Boss says to do, and tries to tell others to act the same way, will not be thought of very highly in heaven, but those cowboys who do what the Boss says to do will be rewarded handsomely in heaven. [20] So listen up, if you can't do better than those fake religious fellows, you won't see hide nor hair of God's Green Pastures.

[21] "You heard that the Boss said long ago, 'Don't kill anyone and if you do, you run the risk of bein' found guilty.' [22] But I'm tellin' you that it's no different if you're even mad at your brother over somethin' stupid. You can still be found just as guilty. Just by callin' someone a fool is reason enough to be tried.

[23] "If you're gonna grab a knee and worship God and you realize that your brother or amigo is mad at ya, [24] get up and track 'em down and get things right between ya'll. Get things straightened out and then come back and offer your prayers.

In verses 1-11, Jesus said that what God thinks is important is different from the world dotes on—to God, helpin' others is very important, but money and power don't mean much. When you think about what is important to you, do you share God's values or the world's values?

In verses 21-22, Jesus said that both killing and being mad enough to kill are wrong—so when it comes to sin, what you do is just as bad as what you ponder. Have you tried to control not only your actions but what you think as well?

[25] "If you deal someone from the bottom of the deck and they decide to file charges on you for your wrongdoing, you better make it up to them before you get thrown in jail. [26] I'm tellin' you that you won't get out before every last penny has been repaid.

[27] "Ya'll have heard that you shouldn't 'jack with someone else's jenny.' [28] But I'm tellin' you that even if you look at a girl and think about it, you've done the same thing in your heart. [29] If you think your eye has a mind of its own, then poke it out with a sharp stick. It's better to have one eye than to burn in hell. [30] If your right hand won't listen to you, lop it off with an axe for the very same reason.

[31] "It's been said that, 'If anyone gets a divorce from his wife, he's gotta give her the papers that say so.' [32] But I'm tellin' you that you better stick with her unless she's been sleepin' around. 'Cause if you don't, you're gonna make an adulteress out of her and anyone that marries her is going to be found guilty of adultery.

[33] "If you remember, the Boss told your grand-daddies, 'Don't go back on your word, but stand behind everything you say to the Lord.' [34] But I'm tellin' you straight, Don't swear at all: either by heaven, for it's the Boss' pasture; [35] or by the earth, for it's the trap around the headquarters; or by Jerusalem, for it's the Boss' headquarters. [36] And don't swear by your own abilities. You can't make even one hair on your head become white or black. [37] It's this simple. Let your 'Yes' mean 'Yes' and your 'No' mean 'No'; anything other than this is the same thing the devil would say.

[38] "You've heard again and again, the old sayin', 'An eye for an eye, and a tooth for a tooth.' [39] But I'm tellin' you right now, don't shoot for revenge against anyone. If someone smacks you on the right cheek, let him have an easy shot at the left one too. [40] If someone wants to steal your vest, give 'em your coat too. [41] If someone makes you walk a mile behind their horse, go even further than that. [42] Give to those that ask and don't turn anyone away when they ask to borrow something.

[43] "You remember that it was said, 'Love your buddies and hate those that hate you.' [44] But I tell you: Love those that hate you and pray for those that run their mouths about you. [45] Then God will claim you as his own son. He makes the sun shine on the good, the bad, and the ugly, and sends 'em all the same rain to boot. [46] If you only love those that love you right back, what kind of love are you really showin'? Even politicians do that! [47] If you only say hi to your brother and your buddies, do you really think you are doin' somethin' special? Even dogs sniff each other's butts when they recognize each other and growl when a strange dog comes by. [48] Be perfect just like the Boss is.

In verses 29-30, Jesus said you should get rid of anything that causes you to get all hot and bothered—which nowadays might mean certain magazines, web sites or even folks in your life. Is there something or someone that makes you act like a young bull turned out with a bunch of heifers that you should cut out of your life?

In verses 43-48, Jesus said you should love both your pards and your enemies—because when you hate someone, you make it impossible to show the love of Christ through you. Is there someone you could bring closer to Christ if you showed them love instead of hate?

Matthew 6

Jesus Continues to Teach

"Don't be a cowboy that only rides his horse in parades so people will notice him. If you do things just so folks will see you, there won't be a reward for you in heaven. [2] If you help out a cowboy in need, don't go around telling everyone about it so they will admire you. I'm dead serious when I say that you will already have received all the notoriety you will ever get if you act that way. [3] But when you do help someone out, don't let the glove on your left hand know what the glove on your right hand is doin'. [4] If you help folks privately, the Boss knows and will reward you himself.

[5] "If you only take your hat off and pray when other people are watching, their appreciation is all you're gonna get. [6] But when you pray, head out to the barn where even the horses can't see you. Then the Boss, who sees and hears everything, will reward you.

[7] "When you talk to the Boss, don't run your mouth off like an auctioneer that don't know when to say 'Sold!' Just repeatin' the same words over and over and over again don't get your prayers answered. [8] Don't be like those kinds of guys, 'cause the Boss knows exactly what you need before you ever open your mouth! [9] This is how you should talk to the Boss:

> Our Boss, who owns the heavenly pastures in the sky, may your name be revered above all others. [10] I hope your pastures come soon and I hope we all do what you want us to down here—just like things are done up there on your spread. [11] Bring us today everything we'll need to get us by, [12] and look the other way when we fail you. Help us also to look the other way when our partners fail us. [13] And don't let us fall into gopher holes that will kill us, but keep us safe and sound from evil.

[14] "If you look the other way when people do you wrong, the Boss will do the same for you. [15] But if you hold grudges against your fellow cowboys, the Boss will treat you the same way.

[16] "If you want to show the Boss how much you care for him by goin' without food

---

In verse 1, Jesus said to do good things for God, not to impress other cowboys, because if you just want to look all high and mighty to other people, then that will be the only reward you get. When you do something good—like giving, praying or fasting—who do you do it for?

for a little while, don't go around tellin' everyone what you're doin'. Those that do are lookin' for sympathy and admiration from everyone but the Boss. That's all they'll get out of it, too. [17] But if you go without food for a while, saddle up and ride just like it's any normal day of work. [18] Then the Boss will know that the only reason you're doin' it is for him. It's this kind of stuff that he rewards.

[19] "Don't buy a bunch of saddles and tradin' spurs here on earth so that people will think highly of you. The saddles will eventually rot and the spurs will rust if someone doesn't break into your barn and steal 'em first. [20] Shoot for the great things of heaven, where there is no rot and thieves can't break in. [21] Whatever you long for the most is where your heart really is.

[22] "Your eye is like the lantern of your body. When your eyes are good, your whole body (or the barn in this case) is filled with light. [23] But when your eyes are bad, the whole barn is filled with darkness. [24] If you mistake darkness for the light, you have a mighty dark barn my friend.

[25] "That's why I'm tellin' you not to worry about anything. Don't worry 'bout food or water, or if you will have boots to wear. Isn't this life more than about beef steaks, and isn't your body more than about boots? [26] Look at the birds. They don't have a herd of cattle to butcher for beef or a garden to pick vegetables for canning, but the Boss provides for them every day. You mean a lot more to him than little birds do. [27] Can a little bit of worry really do anything to add a single moment more to your life?

[28] "Why worry about your boots and chaps? Even prickly pear have apples and grow strong in the pasture. Cactus don't have to work for these beautiful apples, [29] and even the richest man who ever lived, Solomon, didn't have clothes like a cactus does. [30] And if the Boss cares so much for cactus' that are here today and rot tomorrow, he certainly cares for you. Why can't you have a little more faith than that?"

[31] "So don't sit around frettin' all the time, sayin' things like, 'I wonder what we'll eat? Will there be anything to drink? Will I have a neckerchief to keep warm in the winter?' [32] This is the way people think that don't believe in the Boss, but he knows everything you need. [33] Search out his way before you search for anything else, and be sure and live like he wants you to. Then he will give you everything you need.

[34] "Don't fret about tomorrow, for tomorrow will fret about itself. Today's filled with enough frettin' for one day.

In verse 24, Jesus said you can chose only one master, either God or money—although anything that you think about more than God can also be your master. What do you spend most of your time thinking about—God, money or something else?

In verses 25-34, Jesus said you shouldn't fret about the things you need in life, like grub, wrangler jeans, and a roof over your head, because if you ride for God, he will provide for you. Even though you work hard, do you still worry or do you trust God to provide?

Matthew 7

Judging Others

"Don't make opinions about what others do, and no opinion will be made about you. [2] The way you treat others is the way you will be treated. The judging eye you cast upon others will be the same judging eye that will be cast on you.

[3] "Don't criticize your partner's horse for slinging its head when you can't even get on your own horse without gettin' bucked off. [4] How can you offer to help your friend out with his horse when you can't even put a saddle on yours? [5] That's just bein' a hypocrite! When you get your horse goin' good and steady, then you can offer to help your partner.

[6] "Don't give the best of what the Boss has given you to the coyotes. Don't throw pearls into the pig pen just so they will get mashed down in the mud and never be seen again.

How to Talk to the Boss

[7] "If you need somethin', keep tellin' the Boss about it and you will get it. If you keep lookin' for the cows in the pasture, you will find them if you don't give up. If you keep knockin' on the barn door, he will open it for you. [8] If you ask, you will receive. If you knock, the door will be opened. If you look, you will find.

[9] "If you're a mom or a dad, listen up. If your children are hungry and ask for something to eat, do you hand them a fence post? [10] If they ask for some macaroni and cheese, do you give them turpentine and taters? Of course you don't! [11] So if you sinners know how to take care of your kids, how much more will the Boss be able to take care of those he thinks of as his own children?

The Rule to Live By

[12] "Work another man's horse the way you want him workin' your best horse. This is what the Rules and the Wise Cowboys were tryin' to teach all those years ago.

In verses 1-5, Jesus said to take a hard look at yourself before you judge what's wrong with other people. When you are tempted to criticize someone for something, do you check the mirror first to see if you are guilty of the same thing?

The Narrow Sorting Gate

[13] "You can only enter the Boss' ranch by way of the narrow sortin' gate. The trail to hell is wide open and easy to follow for those that choose it. [14] But the gate to life is narrow and the trail is rough and steep. Only a few will ever find it or be able to follow it.

The Mesquite Tree and Its Beans

[15] "Look out for the fake fellows who stop by the ranch disguised as harmless sheep but are really rabid coyotes. [16] You can spot 'em by their beans. Can you pick beans off of tumbleweeds, or taters off of cockleburs? [17] A good tree produces beans that will feed the animals, but a bad tree produces beans that kill cattle and cowboys. [18] A good tree can't make bad beans and a bad tree can't make good beans. [19] So every tree that can't make good beans is cut down and used for firewood. [20] You can spot a tree by its beans, and you can spot people by their ways.

Real Cowboys

[21] "Not everyone who claims to be a cowboy that works for me will end up on the Boss' ranch. Only those cowboys who do what the Boss wants them to will end up there. [22] On the day of reckonin', many cowboys will claim that they worked for me. They will say, 'Lord! Lord! Didn't we ride out and tell people about you and get rid of evil things in your name? Didn't we do things that could only have come from you?' [23] But I'm gonna tell 'em, 'Maybe so! But we never rode together as partners and amigos. Get out of my sight and off my spread.'

Building a House on Solid Rock

[24] "Any cowboy who listens to what I tell them and does it, knows the right trail to take. Just like a cowboy that builds his bunkhouse on solid rock. [25] When the creek rises and the north wind blows like a hurricane, not a thing will happen to it. [26] But anyone who listens to what I'm sayin' and then just blows it off is like the cowboy who built his bunkhouse on sand. [27] When the creek rises and the norther starts blowin', his bunkhouse won't last a split second."

[28] When Jesus was done talkin', everyone just kind of stood there in awe and wonder. [29] He said things like he knew what he was talkin' about and had the authority to say it—unlike those fake fellas that didn't know nothin' except rules and regulations.

In verses 15-20, Jesus said to watch out for sorry teachers, which is anybody that has an influence on how you live, because they are actually more interested in helping themselves than you. Is there someone that has taught you to sling your head?

In verses 24-27, Jesus said that if you build your life around what he says, you will be able to weather the storm—but if you don't, you won't. Do you know people who have used their faith to help them through some deep canyons of life?

13

Matthew 8

Jesus Heals a Man with Hoof Rot

A ton of people followed Jesus as he came down from the mesa. [2] All of a sudden, a man came from the brush and took off his hat and hit one knee right in front of him and said, "Boss, if you want to, you can heal me of this hoof rot."

[3] Jesus laid a hand on the guy's shoulder and said, "I sure enough want to. Be healed!" The hoof rot that had covered his body instantly vanished. [4] Jesus told him, "Don't say a word about this to anyone. Instead, head to town and let the priest have a look at you. Take something with you so you can offer it to God for healin' you. This is how you will let people know you've been healed."

The Brand Inspector's Faith

[5] When Jesus went back to Capernaum, a Roman brand inspector came to him and begged him, [6] "Lord, my young day-worker is paralyzed and in a lot of pain."

[7] Jesus said, "I'll go with you and make him well."

[8] But the brand inspector told him, "I'd really rather you not. It's not necessary. All you have to do is say the word and I know the young lad will be healed. [9] I know this because I do what my boss tells me to and my cowboys that ride for me do what I tell them to. If I give 'em word to ride hard west, they do it. If I give 'em word to come back, they do it."

[10] Jesus stood there amazed. He turned around and said, "That's the kind of faith I've been lookin' for and I finally found it! [11] And let me tell you something else folks. Cowboys and cowgirls are goin' to come from everywhere and sit down at the Great Campfire in the sky with all the saints. [12] But a lot of the cowboys from Israel—those that the Campfire was made for—will be thrown out in the darkness on their heads, where there will be constant squawlin' and grindin' of teeth."

[13] Then Jesus told the brand inspector, "Go on back to your hacienda. Your young cowboy will be healed because you believed I could do it." Come to find out, the young

---

In verses 1-3, Jesus healed a man with leprosy, which was an incurable sickness that could be spread by touch, causing many folks to turn their backs on lepers. If Jesus could help a leper, is there any reason you should turn your back on those that need your help?

In verses 5-13, a soldier showed more faith than the so-called "religious" people—and because of his faith, Jesus did more for that solider than he did for the "religious" people. Which group pleases God more, cowboys who only say they ride the narrow trail or cowboys who really do?

cowboy was healed at that exact hour.

Jesus Cures Many Folks

¹⁴ When Jesus made it back to Peter's house, Peter's mother-in-law was mighty ill with a burnin' fever. ¹⁵ But when Jesus walked in and touched her on the hand, the fever left her. She felt so good she got up and cooked 'em all some buttermilk biscuits.

¹⁶ That evening while they were sittin' on the porch, a bunch of folks were brought to Jesus that were possessed by devilish spirits. Jesus simply told the spirits to take a hike and the people were cured. Jesus also healed everyone that was sick. ¹⁷ This fulfilled what Isaiah had said about him long ago:

> *"He hauled out our sicknesses and vanquished our diseases."*

Following Jesus has its Costs

¹⁸ Jesus saw that the folks were startin' to crowd around him so he told his cowboys to cross to the other side of the lake.

¹⁹ Then one of the teachers that taught the rules said to him, "Hey, I'll go wherever you go Jesus."

²⁰ But Jesus told him, "Coyotes have dens and birds have nests, but the Boss' Son doesn't have any place to call home."

²¹ Another fellow said, "My dad died, and as soon as his funeral's over, I'll come with you."

²² Jesus shook his head and said, "If you are really willin' to follow me then do it right now. You can't help anyone that's already dead."

Jesus and the Storm

²³ Then Jesus jumped in the boat and they headed for the other side of the lake. ²⁴ All of a sudden, a boat-sinker of a storm blew in. But Jesus had his hat down over his eyes and slept through it. ²⁵ The disciples were frettin' and fearin' that this was gonna be the end of them all. They finally woke Jesus up by shakin' him and saying, "Jesus, save us!! We're all gonna drown!"

²⁶ Jesus shook his head patiently and said, "Quit actin' like a bunch of sissies! You ain't got very much faith at all, do you?" Jesus got up, stretched, and told the wind to

---

In verses 14-15, Jesus healed Peter's mom-in-law—and she immediately got up and looked for ways to serve him. The next time God helps you, will you show your appreciations by looking for ways to ride for him as quick as you can?

shut-up and the waves to sit down . . . and they did.

²⁷ The hands were shocked, stunned, and amazed and asked, "What kind of hombre is this? Even the wind and the waves listen at him!"

The Demons and the Pigs

²⁸ When he got over to the Gadarene country, two possessed men that came from the cemetery met him. They was so brutal and mean that no one could pass that way. ²⁹ "What does the Boss' Son want with us?" they screamed. "Have you come to kill us before you are supposed to?"

³⁰ There was a herd of pigs feeding in the next pasture. ³¹ The demons begged and cried out to Jesus, "If you get rid of us, send us into that herd of pigs over there."

³² He told them, "Alright then. Go!" So the demons left the men and went into the herd of pigs. When they possessed the pigs, the four-legged slop eaters all ran to a cliff and jumped in the water and drown. ³³ The farmers that were tendin' the pigs ran off to town and told everyone what had happened, includin' what had happened to the two demon possessed men. ³⁴ Everyone got together when they heard the news and went out to confront Jesus. When they saw him, they told him to get the heck out of Dodge.

Matthew 9

The Man Who Could Not Move

Jesus got in a boat and headed for the town where he was raised. ² Some fellows brought him a guy that was paralyzed and could not move, lying on a bedroll. When Jesus saw their faith, he said to the guy on the bedroll, "Don't worry amigo, your sins are forgiven."

³ Some teachers of the law said to each other, "This fella can't do that and get away with it!"

⁴ Jesus knew what they were thinking and saying. He said to them, "Why are your minds filled with evil? ⁵ What's easier for me to say, 'Your sins are forgiven,' or to say,

---

In verses 1-8, Jesus not only forgave the stove-up man's sins, but he also healed his legs—which he did to prove to the crowd that he had the power he said he had. Are you waiting for Jesus to show you a miracle before you'll ride for him?

'Get up and walk?' ⁶ Just so you know, the Boss' Son can forgive sins here on earth." Then he told the man who couldn't move, "Get up, take your bedroll and mosey on back home." ⁷ The man did just that. ⁸ When everyone saw this, they were amazed and praised the Boss, who had given this type of authority and power to men.

Jesus Sups with Sinners

⁹ When Jesus left there, he saw a guy named Matthew sitting at the Tax Collector's shack. "Come on," he told him and Matthew left everything right there and went with him.

¹⁰ Jesus went to Matthew's house and supped with him. A lot of Matthew's friends, mostly outlaws and politicians that were crooked, came and ate with them and Jesus' hands. ¹¹ When the Religious-Know-It-Alls (Pharisees) seen this, they asked Jesus' cowboys, "Why does your trail boss eat with outlaws and no-accounts?"

¹² Jesus heard 'em and said, "The healthy cattle don't need a Vet, the sick one's do. ¹³ You need to head off and ponder what this means: 'I want mercy, not sacrifice.' Because I haven't come to round up the gentle cattle, but I have come to gather the mavericks."

Religious Leaders Question Jesus about Fasting

¹⁴ John the Baptist's day-workers came and questioned Jesus about worshiping God by not eating. They asked, "Why is it that the Religious-Know-It-Alls (Pharisees) and us fast, but your cowhands don't have to?"

¹⁵ Jesus told them, "The folks at a wedding don't get all sad and mopey when the groom is at the party. There will come a time he has to light out and leave 'em. That's when they will fast."

¹⁶ "You don't put an unshrunk cotton patch on a pair of britches that are torn. As soon as you wash them, the patch will shrink and make the tear worse. ¹⁷ Neither do cowboys put new wine into an old wineskin. New wine will ferment and expand, stretchin' the leather bag. If the bag has already been stretched, it's just gonna tear. That's why you put new wine into new leather wineskins and old wine into old wineskins. That way, both are still usable."

In verse 9, Jesus told Matthew to follow him and Matthew did—leaving behind a job that made him a lot of money by swindlin' folks with their taxes. Is there anything in your life that you need to leave underneath a mesquite bush because it keeps you from following Jesus?

In verses 10-12, Jesus supped with sinners, including Matthew who was a cheating tax collector—yet Matthew would become one of the original twelve disciples of Christ. Have you thought that some people were too rank to follow Jesus—or have you felt like you were one of those cowboys?

Jesus Heals a Couple of Girls

¹⁸ When Jesus was talking, a man that was in charge of running a church came and got down on his knees in front of him. The man said, "My daughter has just died. But I believe if you come to my house, you can raise her from the dead." ¹⁹ Jesus got up immediately and told his hands to come on.

²⁰ Just then, a lady who had been bleeding for twelve years snuck up behind Jesus and touched the edge of his shirt. ²¹ She told herself, "I know I will be healed if I can touch him. Even if it's the edge of his shirt."

²² Jesus spun around and told her, "Cheer up, daughter," he said, "you've just been healed by your faith." From that very moment, the woman was healed.

²³ When Jesus entered the house of the guy whose daughter had died, he saw people cryin' and playin' sad songs on instruments. ²⁴ Jesus told 'em, "This girl ain't dead, she's just asleep." But they all just laughed and mocked him. ²⁵ Jesus told 'em all to get out and when they were all outside, he went into the little girl's bedroom. Jesus went up to her and took her by the hand and she stood up. ²⁶ Word spread around the countryside like wildfire about what had happened.

The Blind and Mute are Healed by Jesus

²⁷ When Jesus left, two blind guys followed him and yelled out to him, "Help us and have mercy on us Son of David!"

²⁸ He took 'em indoors and asked them, "Do you think that I can heal you?"

"Yes, Lord," they said.

²⁹ He reached out and gently touched their eyes and said, "It will be done according to your faith." ³⁰ Just then, their sight was restored. But the first thing they saw was Jesus wagging a stern finger at them. Jesus said, "Don't you tell a soul about this. You understand me?" ³¹ But them fellows went out and told everyone what had happened to them.

³² When Jesus and his cowhands left, a man that was demon possessed and couldn't talk was brought to Jesus. ³³ Jesus drove the demon out and the man spoke for the first time. Those that were watching stood there with their mouths hanging wide open in astonishment. They said, "No one has ever seen anything as awesome as this in all of Israel!"

In verses 36-38 (ahead on page 19), Jesus called the crowd "cattle," meaning many were ready to be brought into God's kingdom—but he also said he needed day-workers to go into those "pastures." Are you prepared for God to use you to gather someone into his kingdom?

[34] But the Religious-Know-It-Alls (Pharisees) said, "He must be working for the devil in order to drive out demons."

Prayer for More Cowboys to Gather Mavericks

[35] Jesus went all throughout the country, teaching in their churches, telling the good news of God's Green Pastures and healing every ache and ailment. [36] When he saw all the mavericks, he felt sorry for them because they were shunned and starved, like cattle without a brand and no rancher to take care of 'em. [37] Then he told his cowboys, "The cattle are everywhere, but there just ain't enough cowboys. [38] Ask the Lord of the gathering to send out cowboys into his pastures."

Matthew 10

Jesus Sends His Cowboys Out to Gather

Jesus hollered for his cowboys to come over to him. He gave 'em the authority to get rid of evil spirits and to cure ills and ailments.

[2] These are the names of the first cowhands (apostles): Peter and his brother Andrew; old Zebedees' sons James and John; [3] Phillip and Bart (sometimes called Bartholomew); Thomas and the tax collector Matthew; Alphaeus' boy James, and Thad (also called Thaddaeus by his grandma); [4] Simon, who was extremely intense, and Judas Iscariot, who double-crossed Jesus.

[5] Jesus sent these twelve cowboys out to gather and laid out for them what he wanted them to do: "Don't go to the pastures that aren't Jewish just yet or any pastures where the cross-bred Samaritans hang out. [6] Go gather the lost cattle of Israel. [7] When you're out there, give everyone this message: 'The kingdom of heaven and the Boss' perfect pastures are real close.' [8] Doctor anyone that is sick and I'm even givin' you the gift of raisin' up those that are dead. You didn't do anything to deserve any of this and you should give just as I have given you. [9] Don't hide any cash or coins in the bottom of your boots; [10] take no saddle bags or bedrolls, or an extra vest or pair of britches; those you take care of will and should take care of you.

In verse 1, Jesus "called" his apostles, which means he invited them—he didn't rope 'em and drag them to him; he let them decide for themselves. Which choice have you been making—to follow Jesus or to stay behind?

In verse 2-4, among the people called to be apostles, there were fishermen, a tax collector and a political activist—people from all walks of life. If Jesus can use a man who works with fish or taxes or politics, don't you think he can use one that works with horses?

¹¹ "It don't matter whether you're stayin' at a ranch, a town, or a big city, find someone honest and trustworthy and stay at their place until you leave. ¹² When you enter the home, take your hat off to it. ¹³ If the place and its people treat you well and deserves your blessin', give it to 'em. If not, don't feel bad about takin' it with you. ¹⁴ If no one welcomes you in or listens to what you say, shake the dust off your boots and ride away. ¹⁵ I'm tellin' you what, it'll be better for Sodom and Gomorrah on judgment day than it will be for that place. ¹⁶ I'm sendin' ya'll out like steaks to hungry coyotes. Ya'll will need to be savvy as horse traders, but innocent as the day you were born.

Jesus Tells His Cowboys About the Coming Rough Times

¹⁷ "Watch your backs with men. They will hand you over to the local sheriffs and beat you within an inch of your life, right there in the churches. ¹⁸ Because of me, you will be taken before governors, presidents, and later, even to those who aren't Jews, so that you can tell them about who I am. ¹⁹ Don't fret about what you're supposed to say when they arrest you though. When the time comes, I'll give you the words that you'll need. ²⁰ It won't be you that'll be talkin' at 'em, it'll be the Spirit of God speakin' through you.

²¹ "Brothers are gonna double-cross each other, and a father will do the same to his kid. Children will buck their parents and turn on 'em, and have 'em put to death. ²² Everyone will hate you because of me, but if you stay in the saddle and ride with me, you will be saved in the end. ²³ When they pester, plague, pick-on, and persecute you, just saddle up and ride away to somewheres else. I'm tellin' you honest, you won't even get through the towns of Israel before the Son of Man comes.

²⁴ "A cowhand isn't over the trail boss and a horse isn't above its rider. ²⁵ It's fine for the cowhand to be like the trail boss. If the trail boss has been called Satan, then his crew will be called that more!

²⁶ "So don't fret or be afraid of them. Nothin' will be hidden where you won't see it comin'. ²⁷ What I tell you around the campfire at night, tell everyone else durin' the day. What I whisper to you in private, tell the whole world. ²⁸ Don't be scared of people that can kill your body. They can't kill your soul. Instead, be afraid of the one that can kill your body and soul in hell. ²⁹ You can buy two little birds for a penny, can't you? But not one of them will fall out of the sky without God's permission. ³⁰ He even knows how many hairs you have underneath your hat. ³¹ What I'm sayin' is, don't be afraid of anything. The Boss loves you a lot more than little birds.

³² "If you tell everyone at the livery, the feed store, the cow sale, the boot shop, and

---

In verse 16, Jesus told the disciples to tell people the good news about him, but be prepared for people who would try to mistreat them or take advantage of them. The next time you share the Gospel with someone, will you remember to be as savvy as a snake but as innocent as a dove?

In verse 32, Jesus said that if a person would speak up for him to other men, he would speak up for that person to God—but if a person would not speak up for him, then neither would he speak up for them. When is the last time you spoke up for Jesus?

anywhere else you go, that you belong to my crew, I will tell God that you ride with me. [33] But if you deny ridin' with me, I'll dang sure deny you before the Boss when you get there.

[34] "Don't think that I have come to make everyone lovey-dovey and peaceful. I didn't come to bring superficial harmony, but a sword. [35] Because I have come to turn 'a boy against his dad, a girl against her mom, a daughter-in-law against her husband's mother—[36] a cowboy's worst enemies will be the folks on his own spread.'

[37] "Any cowboy that loves his mom or dad more than me isn't worthy to ride for my outfit. Same goes for anyone who loves their kids more than they love me. [38] Anyone who isn't willin' to take up his own cross and ride with me isn't worthy of me. [39] Anyone that rides for themselves will lose their life, but whoever rides with me and shuns themselves for my sake will find life.

[40] "He who welcomes and receives you receives me, and he who receives me receives the Boss. [41] Anyone who welcomes one of my cowboys gets the same reward as the cowboy that rides for me and anyone who welcomes an honest man because he is honest will get an honest man's bounty. [42] And if someone so much as lifts a finger to help one of my cowboys because they ride for me, I'm tellin' you straight, he will get rewarded."

Matthew 11

John's Bout with Doubt

When Jesus got through training on his cowboys, he went and trained others that would listen in and around Galilee.

[2] John the Baptist was stuck in jail and when he heard all the great things Jesus was accomplishin', [3] he sent some of his boys out to ask Jesus, "Are you the real deal or should we be waitin' on someone else?"

[4] Jesus said, "Go back and tell John what you see and hear: [5] The blind have been cured, the lame are walkin' around, those with all sorts of diseases are bein' cured, deaf ears can now hear, folks are comin' back from the dead, and the good news is

---

In verses 2-3, John started to doubt Jesus, and Jesus said to look at the facts—Jesus healed the blind, the lame, the lepers, the deaf and the dead, all while spreading the good news. If you start to doubt Jesus, will you look at the facts in the Bible and in the changed lives of Christian cowboys?

bein' taught to the poor. [6] God will bless those who won't shy away or be ashamed of ridin' with me."

[7] When John's boys left, Jesus began tellin' everyone that was there about John. "What kind of man did y'all think would be livin' out there in the desert? Someone that resembles a tumbleweed and is just blown around the pasture every time the wind picks up? [8] Did you go out there lookin' for a guy in a three-piece suit? Those guys live in fancy houses, not the desert. [9] If you went out there lookin' for a prophet, then you sure enough found him. But John was more than just a prophet, [10] he is the one that they've been talkin' about since before you were born:

> 'I'm sendin' a cowboy to blaze a trail for you, and he will bust the brush open so you can come through.'

[11] "This right here's the truth: No woman has ever given birth to someone greater than John the Baptist. But, the sorriest cowboy in God's Green Pastures is greater than John. [12] From the days of John the Baptist until right now, the Pastures of Heaven have been ridin' this way hard and many ruthless people have been attacking it. [13] Until John came, all the world had been waitin' and talkin' and lookin' forward to this time right here. [14] If you'll open your minds and hearts to understand this, he is just like the great cowboy Elijah, who wasn't scared to tell folks the truth and tell them about me comin'. [15] If you got a lick of sense you'll be able to understand what I'm tellin' you.

[16] "Let me see if I can explain the folks of this generation. They are like the fans in the stands while the cowboys stand in the arena and talk to them. The cowboys say to them:

> [17] We rode the rough stock for you and got bucked off, but you didn't cheer because you wanted to see us rope. We roped fast and quick, but you didn't clap because no one got bucked off."

[18] "John didn't drink alcohol and often went without food so he could pray, but y'all said he was evil. [19] But then I come, the Son of Man, having a beer with outlaws and whores but y'all say, 'He's a pig and a drunk and he hangs out with low lifes.' A wise man gets results no matter what."

Rest for the Soul is Coming

[20] Jesus began to criticize the cities where most of his miracles had been done. Even after all he did, they just kept right on with their same old sorry ways instead of ridin'

In verse 25 (ahead on page 23), Jesus prayed about two kinds of people—the worldly "wise" who think they have all the answers and the "children" of God who look to God for wisdom. Which one are you—the arrogant know-it-all or the humble child of God?

with him. ²¹ "Oh what a heavy price that Korazin and Bethsaida are gonna have to pay. If the miracles that had been done there had been done in Tyre or Sidon, they would have stopped all their sinning and given glory to God. ²² I'm serious when I say that Tyre and Sidon will be a lot better off on judgment day than for y'all. ²³ And don't even get me started on Capernaum! Your trail ain't headed north, it's at a dead run to the south. If the miracles that had been performed for you had been done in Sodom, those cowboys would still be around and ridin' for me. ²⁴ Sodom is gonna fair a lot better on judgment day than you are Capernaum."

²⁵ That's when Jesus said, "Thank you God for hiding all these things from the know-it-alls and the pompous wise men, and showin' it all to little kids. ²⁶ Yup! This is the way that you wanted it.

²⁷ "My Father has given me everything. Nobody knows me like my Father does, and nobody knows my Father like I do, except for those cowboys and cowgirls that I choose to show who he really is.

²⁸ "Come and ride with me, all of y'all that are worn smooth out and feel like a miner's old pack mule, and I will take the load off of you and let you lie down in tall green grass. ²⁹ Ride with me and learn what I teach you, 'cause I'm a gentle trail boss and my heart is pure and humble. With me is where you'll find rest for your soul. ³⁰ Ridin' for me is easy, and workin' for me ain't hard either."

Matthew 12

Jesus Works on the Day of Rest

Jesus rode through a wheat field on the day that God had told everyone to relax and rest. His cowboys were famished and picked some of the grain to eat. ² When the Religious-Know-It-Alls saw this, they said to Jesus, "Look at that! Your cowboys are breakin' God's law and workin' on the day he told us to rest."

³ He answered, "Haven't you heard what David did when his crew was hungry? ⁴ He entered God's church, and all of them ate the food that had been left there as offering to God. They weren't supposed to do that. Only the priests are supposed to eat that food. ⁵ When everyone else is supposed to be resting, the priests and preachers are

---

In verses 28-30, Jesus told the people who were tired and stressed-out to find strength and peace in him—because he would show them how to get free of their own pack saddles by living for God. When you feel the need to lighten your load, will you shift your focus from yourself to God?

up working and teachin' everyone else, but they are innocent? ⁶ I'm tellin' you that someone better than a church building is standin' right here. ⁷ Religious hypocrites don't ever understand these words, 'I want a relationship, not a religion'. ⁸ The Son of Man is Boss over the day of rest."

⁹ Then Jesus rode into their church, ¹⁰ and there was a fellow there that had a deformed hand. Tryin' to catch Jesus in a trap, they asked him, "Is it wrong to heal on the day of rest?"

¹¹ Jesus told 'em, "If you had a baby calf that fell in a wash down by the creek and it couldn't get out, wouldn't you rope it and pull it out even if it was the Day of Rest? ¹² Cowboys mean a lot more to God than calves do! There ain't nothin' wrong with healin' on the Day of Rest."

¹³ Then he told the guy with the deformed hand, "Take your hand out of your pocket and hold it over here." The guy did what he was told and Jesus healed it completely. ¹⁴ The Religious-Know-It-Alls got so dad-gummed mad at Jesus for doin' this that they started ponderin' how they might take him out.

Folks Flock to Jesus

¹⁵ Jesus knew they was gonna try to take him out, so he left. A huge herd of folks followed him when he left and he healed all that were sick, ¹⁶ but he told 'em all not to tell anyone who did it. ¹⁷ This was because the great cowboy Isaiah had seen the future when he wrote:

> ¹⁸ *"Look here at the guy that works for me, the cowboy that I love and the one I have chosen. I will give my power to him and he will bring justice to the whole world.*
>
> ¹⁹ *He will not squabble or raise his voice in public.*
>
> ²⁰ *He won't ride his horse over the weak and pitiful, nor will he dash the smallest dream until he conquers the world with his final showdown.*
>
> ²¹ *His name will become the hope of the whole world."*

²² Then the people brought him a possessed man that couldn't talk or see. Jesus healed him completely so that he was no longer possessed, nor blind or mute. ²³ Everyone was dumbfounded by the things that Jesus did and they asked, "Could this cowboy be the Son of David?"

In verses 1-13, Jesus condemned the religious leaders who used the Good Book to control people rather than encourage them. Do you know someone who uses the Bible to put people down more often than they use it to help people "get back on"?

²⁴ But when the Religious-Know-It-Alls heard them ask this, they said, "Jesus can only do this because he has Satan's power!"

²⁵ Jesus knew what they were thinkin' and said, "Any crew that is divided won't be able to get the job done. You can't pull on the reins and spur at the same time and expect to get anywhere. ²⁶ If the devil drives himself out, he won't be able to do his job. ²⁷ If I drive out demons by the devil's power, by what power do y'all drive them out? Y'alls followers are doin' the same thing I am, so what does that say about them? ²⁸ But if I bust demons out of people by the Power of God, then that means that God is right here with ya.

²⁹ "Let's go on with this a little longer. How can you take a badger's babies without getting bit? If you shoot the mama, then you'll be able to take her babies.

³⁰ "If you don't ride with me, you are my enemy. If you don't gather with me, then you scatter what I am tryin' to do. ³¹ I'm tellin' you straight that every sin and wrong doing will be forgiven except sinning against the Power of God. ³² You can talk trash about me and it will be forgiven. But if you say that the Spirit of God is just hogwash, you will never want to ride with me or believe in God. For this, you will not be forgiven—in this time, or any time that comes.

³³ "A cow is judged on what kind of calf she throws. Make a cow healthy and she will throw a healthy calf. If a cow is unhealthy or sick, she will have a sick calf. ³⁴ Y'all Know-It-Alls are a den of snakes! How can a snake tell someone what is good? Whatever is in your heart will spill up and out of your mouth. ³⁵ A good cowboy will bring good things up out of his good heart without even knowing it, and the evil man will throw up his nastiness on everyone around and not think anything about it. ³⁶ But I'm warnin' you the next time you let your tongue slip, you will have to explain every single slip and careless word on judgment day. ³⁷ Your words today will affect your outcome when you die. They will either get you turned out on perfect pastures or get you shipped off on the killer truck."

Religious Leaders Want a Miracle

³⁸ Some of the Know-It-Alls and legalistic teachers said to Jesus, "Mr. Teacher, we want to see one of these miracles we keep hearin' about."

³⁹ He answered them, "Only wicked folks who don't believe ask for proof of who I am. The only miracle you will see is the same one that happened to the great godly cowboy Jonah. ⁴⁰ He spent three days and nights in the belly of a big catfish. I will

In verse 30, Jesus said that whoever does not ride with him is against him—because anyone that is not following Jesus is rejecting Jesus. Since there are only two outfits to choose from, which side have you chosen to be on: God's or Satan's?

spend three days and nights in the belly of the earth. [41] When Jonah got out of the fish, he went to Nineveh and told them to quit behavin' like they were or they were goin' to hell. That city listened to him and turned to God. Now standin' before you is a cowboy greater than Jonah and you still don't believe. [42] Even the Queen of Sheba, who didn't even know who God was, came and asked Solomon where he got his great wisdom. She listened to him and believed. She will rise up and not speak favorably of all of y'all when judgment day comes because you do not believe or change after you've heard the truth. Now one greater and wiser than Solomon is standing here and you still refuse to believe."

[43] "When I chase the wolf out of your henhouse, it goes out and searches for another place to eat. [44-45] When it can't find anything to eat, it returns with its whole pack and finds your henhouse standing wide open. This is what happens when men are cleaned up, but don't start ridin' for God. They end up worse than when they started."

Jesus Tells Who His Real Family Is

[46] While Jesus was still talkin' to folks, his momma and his brothers waited outside to talk to him. [47] Someone said, "Hey, your momma and your brothers are waiting outside. They want to talk to you."

[48] Jesus told him, "Who do you think my mom and brothers are?" [49] He turned to his twelve cowboys and said, "My brothers and mother are sittin' right here with me. [50] Anyone that rides for my Father's Brand is my real family."

Matthew 13

Planting Alfalfa

Later on that afternoon, Jesus left the bunkhouse and rode down to the pens. [2] There were a bunch of cowboys standing around waitin' on him. He climbed up on the pipe pens where everyone could see him and [3] he started tellin' stories like this one:

"There was a big ranch that had their own farmin' operation. [4] They planted alfalfa and some of the seed fell on the two-track ranch road. Some blue quail came along and ate it right up. [5] Some other seed fell in a rocky area, [6] but them rocks acted like ovens

---

In verses 43-45, Jesus said that leading a clean life is not enough if you are not following God—because if you are not focused on God, Satan can easily distract you and ruin your life. Have you thought that being good was good enough, or did you know you needed God to keep clean?

and cooked the alfalfa right there on the stalk before it could grow very big. ⁷ Still other seed fell among a prickly pear cactus part of the pasture. That durn cactus choked it out 'fore it ever had a chance. ⁸ But some of that alfalfa seed fell on good, fertile soil. This seed produced about ten tons per acre. ⁹ Is anyone here catchin' what I'm sayin'?"

¹⁰ His cowboys came up to him and asked Jesus, "How come you just tell stories to people?"

¹¹ He nodded in understandin' and said, "You can understand these stories, but some cannot. These stories reveal the true nature of God's Green Pastures. ¹² Cowboys that are willin' to listen and try to understand the real meaning behind the stories will be trusted with secrets that others will not be. But those that won't listen, everything will be taken from 'em. ¹³ I tell these cowboy stories because they see what I do, but they don't really see anything at all. They're lookin', but they don't see. They hear the stories, but they're not even listening. They understand, but they don't savvy. ¹⁴ This is why the great cowboy Isaiah said,

> 'You hear, but you don't listen. You see, but you don't understand. ¹⁵ The hearts of the cowboys have become calloused. Their ears don't hear and their eyes don't see. Therefore they can't ride with me and let me fix what ails them.'

¹⁶ "But the blindfold has been taken off of you and the plugs taken out of your ears. ¹⁷ I'm tellin' you, many a cowboy wished to see what you've seen and hear what you've heard, but they could not.

¹⁸ "Now let me tell you what the alfalfa story really means: ¹⁹ The seed that fell on the ranch road are like those cowboys that hear the Good News, but they don't understand it. The Killer then comes and eats the seed away before it can grow in their hearts. ²⁰ The rocky ground is like those cowboys that hear the Good News and take it home with them gladly. ²¹ But the first time it gets a little hot around the collar, they wilt. ²² The seeds that fell in the cactus are like those that hear and accept the Good News, but then they shove the message out of their lives with the cares of this world and the lure of money. ²³ The good soil is like those cowboys that really accept my words. These cowboys will produce tons of harvest for my sake.

The Registered Cattle and the Cull Bull

²⁴ Here's another cowboy story that Jesus told: "God's Green Pasture is like a rancher that had a herd of registered Angus cattle. ²⁵ But when the cows were all comin' into

In verses 18-23, Jesus described four kinds of people who hear the Word: 1) those that don't try to understand it, 2) those that only try to understand a little of it, 3) those that understand it but get distracted from it and 4) those that understand it, ponder it and nod for the gate. Which one are you?

season, the Counterfeit came and put an old mangy, ugly, half Holstein, half Watusi, half buffalo bull in the pasture with the registered herd. ²⁶ When calving time came, some of the cows produced fine, pure-bred Angus calves. But some cows produced an ugly, scrawny calf not worth nothing. ²⁷ The cowboys went and told the rancher that another bull must have got to the cows.

²⁸ That no-account Counterfeit must have done this to me!' the rancher said.

'Do you want us to shoot the cross bred calves?' the cowboys asked.

²⁹ He told them, 'No! You might hit one of the good calves. I've seen your shootin'. ³⁰ Let all of 'em grow up and we'll sort 'em out during shippin' season. That's when I'll tell the sorters to pen them up and burn 'em.'"

The Bull Seed

³¹ Here's another one of Jesus' tales: "God's Green Pasture is like the seed of a bull. ³² It's so small you can't even see it, but when it is planted in the right spot, it grows and becomes the biggest thing in the pasture one day. It is the protector of the herd and won't let anything harm those it looks after."

The Sourdough Starter

³³ Jesus told 'em this: "The Boss' ranch is like a sourdough starter used by the chuckwagon cook to make biscuits. Even though the starter is the smallest part, it works its way through the flour and other ingredients to make the biscuits what they were meant to be."

³⁴ Jesus constantly used stories like these when he talked to the cowboys and cowgirls. Truth be known, he never spoke to them in any other way. ³⁵ This was because many, many moons ago, it was said,

> "I will speak to you in cowboy stories. I will explain mysteries hidden since the beginnin' of time."

The Registered Cattle and Cull Bull Explained

³⁶ Jesus left the day-workers outside and went into the bunkhouse with his cowboys. They sat down on the bunks and asked him to explain the story about the registered cattle and the cull bull.

[37] "All right," he said. "I am the registered bull that makes everything pure. [38] The pasture where the cattle lived is like this old world we're living in right now. The pure bred calves are like the cowboys that live for the Boss. The cull calves are people that follow the Counterfeit. [39] The enemy who put the cull bull in the pasture is the Devil, or you might know him as Slick, or the Counterfeit one. Shippin' season is when this old world will end. The sorters will be the angels.

[40] "Just like the cull calves are sorted out and burned, so it will be in the end. [41] I will send my winged riders to take away anything in my pasture that is not pure and from me. [42] They will throw the culls into the brandin' fire and burn them up. On that day there will be a lot of bawlin' and pain. [43] Then those that are pure because of me will shine like the noon-day sun. If you got ears, ya better listen close to this and understand!

The Unknown Oilfield

[44] "The Boss' ranch is like a cowboy finding oil comin' up out of the ground in an old useless pasture. In his excitement, the cowboy told no one and went and sold every single thing he owned and bought the property.

The Horse Trader

[45] "Again, the Boss' ranch is like a horse trader on the lookout for the best horse he could find. [46] When he discovered the best filly he had ever seen, he sold all his trucks, trailers, and every horse he owned just to get this one.

The Prescribed Pasture Burn

[47] "Are you listening yet? Once again, the Boss' ranch is like cowboys gatherin' the cattle before a prescribed pasture burn. [48] The cowboys only take the cattle that belong to the rancher and leave everything else. [49] This is the way it will be at the end of the world. The winged riders will come down and gather everything that belongs to the Boss and leave everything else. [50] Fire will be set to the pasture and everything left will burn. There will be no escape. [51] Do ya understand what I'm sayin'?"

"Yes sir! We sure enough do," the disciples said.

[52] Then Jesus said, "Every teacher of the Law who starts ridin' for me is like a cowboy who teaches the old way, but isn't afraid to teach something new.

In verse 44, Jesus said the kingdom of heaven is like a treasure that is worth so much, a man would hock everything else he owns in order to buy it. What is the most valuable thing in your life—and how do you compare it to your partnership with God?

Jesus Rejected in His Hometown

⁵³ When Jesus had finished telling his tales, he left that part of the country and went back home. ⁵⁴ He returned to Nazareth and did some teachin' in the local church. Everyone kept wondering where he got such great understandin' and how he performed the miracles. ⁵⁵ They said, "He's just a cowboy's son. We know his whole family. ⁵⁶ His sisters live right here in town. What makes him think he's somethin' special?" ⁵⁷ They all got ticked off at Jesus and refused to believe a word he said.

Then Jesus told 'em, "A preacher is honored everywhere except his hometown and by everyone except his family."

⁵⁸ And so Jesus didn't do much around there like he did other places because they didn't believe in him.

Matthew 14

When old King Herod heard 'bout Jesus, ² he said, "This must be the ghost of John the Baptist come back to life." ³ Herod's wife had conned the King into throwin' John in the juzgow. ⁴ John had told the King that it was wrong for him to marry his brother's wife. ⁵ The King would have killed him right away, but he was afraid that there might be an uprising against him because John was a prophet.

⁶ At Herod's birthday bash, his wife's daughter danced a jig that really impressed the King. ⁷ Herod told her that she could have anything she wanted because she had danced so well. ⁸ At her momma's bidding, she asked the King for the head of John the Baptist.

⁹ Herod was plum tore up about this and didn't know what to do. He'd given his word and he couldn't back down from that.

¹⁰ So John's head was chopped off ¹¹ and brought on a tray to the daughter who then took it to her momma.

¹² John's crew then came and laid claim to his body and went and buried it on Boot Hill. Then they went and told Jesus what had happened.

¹³ When Jesus heard the news, he rode off out into the pasture to be alone. But a

---

In verse 58, Jesus did only a few miracles in his hometown, because the people did not have faith in him—likely, being blind to the fact that he was the Lord kept them from asking for miracles. Could a lack of faith have kept you from seeing miracles God has performed in your life?

In verses 9-10, although the King knew it was wrong to kill John, he did it anyway because he didn't want to be embarrassed in front of his amigos. Have you done something you knew was wrong to earn favor with friends—or have you done something right even though they poked fun at you?

bunch of people saw him ride out and they followed him.

[14] When Jesus got back from his ride, he felt sorry for all those that had gathered and waited on him. He took pity on 'em and healed all that were ailing.

[15] When the sun was goin' down, Jesus' crew came up and told him to send everyone back to town so they could get 'em some supper. [16] But Jesus said that it weren't necessary. "Y'all feed 'em."

[17] They all looked at him like he'd growed donkey ears. "All we got to feed with is five biscuits and two small catfish."

[18] "Bring 'em over here," Jesus said. [19] He told everyone to hunker down while he said grace over the food. He asked God's blessing over the meager meal and then broke the biscuits apart. The cowboys were told to take some to everybody. [20] By the time everyone was finished eating, they were all layin' up under the mesquites as full as ticks. There was even twelve baskets of food left over. [21] There was over 5,000 cowboys there, not counting women-folk and kiddos.

[22] Jesus told his cowboys to go load up in a boat and head home while he made sure everyone else made it back to town. [23] When they had all left, he rode up on a mountain so he could be alone and pray.

[24] By this time, the boys were way out in the middle of this huge lake and a big storm had come up. This storm was a poundin' the tar out of everything and the cowboys were scared. [25] A little while later, Jesus came out of the storm walkin' right across the water. [26] The cowboys saw him and thought for sure that a ghost was comin' for 'em. They started screamin' and bellerin' like the end was near.

[27] Jesus hollered for 'em to relax and said, "Don't worry fellas!! It's me, Jesus. Don't be afraid."

[28] Peter hollered back at him, "Jesus, if it's really you, tell me to walk out there on that water and come to you."

[29] Jesus smirked and said, "Come on then." Peter stood up and walked right off the boat and strode right out there on the water.

[30] But Pete seen the lightning and how the wind was makin' waves and he got scared all over again and began to sink. "Ohhh no!! Help me Jesus! Help me, I'm a sinkin' down!"

In verses 19-21, the disciples had only five loaves of bread and two fishes to offer to Jesus—but with that, Jesus fed over 5,000 with 12 baskets of food left over. Have you held off doing something for God because you felt like what you had to offer to him was too small?

In verse 23, Jesus took time out of his ride every day to pray to God—notice that, even though Jesus was the Son of God, he still set aside a time to talk to God. Whether you are asking God for help or thanking him for your blessings, do you set aside a time each day to talk with God?

³¹ Jesus walked over to him and grabbed him by the shirt collar and said, "Your faith wouldn't fill a thimble. How come you doubt me?"

³² When Jesus got both of 'em over to the shore, the wind died down and the lightning stopped. ³³ The cowboys huddled underneath a mesquite got down on their knees and said, "You are most certainly God's Boy!"

Jesus Heals Some Sick Folks

³⁴ Jesus and his cowboys rode into the town of Gennesaret. ³⁵ The folks found out that he was there and sent word to everyone in the county that Jesus and his boys were there. Sick folks came from miles around so Jesus would make 'em better. ³⁶ They begged Jesus to just let 'em touch his boots, and everyone that did was made well.

Matthew 15

It was about this time that some Religous-Know-It-Alls and some others that taught the same things they did came up from the Jerusalem country. They asked Jesus, ² "Why don't your cowboys do what all of our grandpappies taught us to do? Why, they don't even wash their hands before they eat."

³ Jesus told 'em, "Let me ask you this. Why don't you do what the Boss tells you to do? ⁴ Didn't he tell us to respect our moms and dads? He even said to shoot someone dead if they cussed their parents. ⁵ But y'all let it slide when someone doesn't even help their parents out when they need some help. Y'all tell these kids that it's fine to give money to your organization instead of buying food for their parents. ⁶ Is this the kind of respect that you show your mom and dad? You flat out ignore what the Boss says and make up your own rules that will benefit you! ⁷ Y'all ain't nothin' but snake-oil salesmen! Old Isaiah was tellin' the truth when God spoke through him and said,

> ⁸ 'All of you have real pretty words for me, but I never even cross your mind. ⁹ Don't even bother with your words when all you do is teach rules that you make up.'"

In verses 28-31, Peter walked on water to Jesus—which was a sign of great faith—but he became fretful by the waves, took his eyes off Jesus and began to sink. Where do you look when wrecks happen—the thing causing trouble or the God who can bring you peace?

In verse 1, the religious leaders were adding to God's laws—they thought their traditions were as important as God's instructions. Have you known religious people who believed that their way of doin' things were as important as God's rules?

What Really Makes Cowboys Unfit

[10] Jesus hollered for everyone to gather around him. He said, "Y'all listen up and try to follow what I'm sayin'. [11] The food you put in your mouth doesn't make you unfit in the Boss' eye, but the filthy talk that comes out of your mouth sure enough does."

[12] Some of Jesus' cowboys came over to him and whispered, "Do you realize that you put a big burr underneath them hypocritical preacher's saddle blankets by what you just said?"

[13] Jesus said, "Every animal that doesn't bear the Boss' brand will be shipped off to the slaughter house. [14] Stay away from them hypocritical preachers. They are like blind city slickers leading blind people on blind horses off the edge of a cliff.

[15] Pete asked Jesus, "What was you talkin' about when you said there are things that make a person unfit in the Boss' eyes?"

[16] Jesus told him, "Don't any of you have a clue what I was talkin' about? [17] Don't you understand that anything you put in your mouth goes into your belly and will eventually find its way out of your body? [18] But the words that come out of your mouth come from your heart. These words are what will make you unfit accordin' to the Boss. [19] Out of your heart comes the awful things like: killing, cheatin' on your spouse, gross sexual excitement, horse thieving, goin' back on your word, and talkin' crap about other people. [20] These are the things that the Boss don't like and these are the things that make you unfit."

Real Faith

[21] Jesus shucked out and headed for the country around Tyre and Sidon. [22] All of a sudden, a lady from Canaan shouted out, "Jesus, help me! My daughter is full of evil spirits." [23] Jesus never said a word to her but just kept riding. The lady wouldn't give up, so the cowboys asked Jesus if he would tell her to shut up and leave.

[24] Jesus finally told her, "I was sent only to the cowboys of Israel! They are like a herd of maverick cattle."

[25] The lady came up close to his horse and then got down on her knees and begged, "Please, you're the only one that can help my daughter!"

In verse 14, Jesus said that lost people who follow bad leaders are blind people lead by blind trail guides—and both of them would suffer because of it. Have you had trouble in your life because you followed someone who didn't follow God?

[26] Jesus said, "It isn't right to take a horse away from a cowboy and give it to a city slicker."

[27] "That is true my Lord," she said, "but even city slickers are given one ride by a gentle cowboy."

[28] Jesus smiled and said, "Lady, you've got a passel of faith and you'll be given what you asked for." At that very moment her daughter was made well.

Jesus Keeps On Healing

[29] When he left there, Jesus rode along the shore of Lake Galilee. He rode his horse up on top of a hill and sat there. [30] A whole mess of folks came up there where he was and brought with them people who were in bad shape. Some were blind. Some were deaf. Some were paralyzed and others couldn't talk. They brought 'em before Jesus and he fixed 'em all. [31] Everyone was shocked by what Jesus was able to do. The paralyzed were walkin' and the mutes were talkin'. Everyone was shoutin' and shootin' up in the air in honor of the Boss.

Jesus Gives Sup to 4,000

[32] Jesus called his cowboys over to him and said, "I feel sorry for all these people. They have been here with us for three days and some of 'em haven't had anything to eat. If some of 'em leave, they might pass out before they get home."

[33] His cowboys said, "Man, this place is like a barren desert. We could butcher 100 cows and not have enough food for all these people."

[34] Jesus asked 'em what kind of food they had and they showed him seven small biscuits and some sardines.

[35] Jesus hollered for everyone to sit down and then [36] he took the seven biscuits and the can of sardines and gave thanks for them. He then broke them and handed 'em to his cowboys so they could pass 'em out to everybody.

[37] Everyone ate as much as they wanted and there was enough leftovers to fill seven large dutch ovens.

[38] There were 4,000 cowboys who ate, not counting the women folk and little ones.

[39] After he sent everyone home with their bellies full, Jesus and his crew got on a

---

In verses 23-28, the disciples were annoyed by a woman who repeatedly called for help, so they asked Jesus to send her away, but Jesus helped her instead. When someone asks for your help, do you feel bothered or do you grab the chance to do God's work?

ferry and went to the other side of the lake near the town of Magadon.

Matthew 16

Everyone Wants a Sign

The Hypocritical Preachers (Pharisees) and Cattle Barons (Sadducees) came to Jesus askin' for a sign from the Boss.

[2] He told 'em: "If the sky is red in the evening, you would say that the weather will be good. [3] But if the sky is red and cloudy in the morning you'd say it was about to rain. You're good at lookin' at the weather by the signs in the sky, but you won't open your eyes to what's happenin' right before your eyes. [4] You want proof of the Boss because you are full of evil. The only sign you'll be given is what happened to old Jonah." Then Jesus rode out of town.

The Yeast

[5] The cowboys had forgotten to bring biscuits when they crossed the lake. [6] Jesus warned 'em against the yeast of the Hypocritical Preachers and the Cattle Barons.

[7] The cowboys talked among themselves and said to each other, "He must be sayin' that because we forgot the biscuits."

[8] Jesus knew what they were thinking and said, "Y'all ain't got a lick of faith do you? Why are you talkin' about not havin' any biscuits? [9] Why don't you understand? Did you already forget about those five thousand people and all the leftovers from just five biscuits? [10] And what about the four thousand cowboys and all the leftovers from just seven pieces of hard tack? [11] Don't you know by now I ain't talkin' about biscuits? Watch out for the yeast of the Hypocritical Preachers and Cattle Barons!"

[12] Finally it began to sink in and the cowboys knew what he was talkin' about. He wasn't talkin' about yeast for makin' biscuits, but the things that the Hypocritical Preachers and Cattle Barons tried to get people to do.

In verses 1-4, the religious leaders asked Jesus to perform a miracle before they would believe in him—yet Jesus had already performed many miracles and still they did not believe in him. Are you still asking Jesus to prove himself to you?

Who is Jesus?

¹³ When Jesus and his crew were near the town of Caesarea Phillipi, he asked them, "So what do people say about the Son of the Boss?"

¹⁴ The cowboys looked around and said, "Some people say you are John the Baptist or maybe even the great cowboy Elijah. Others say Jeremiah while some just say you're a prophet."

¹⁵ Then Jesus asked, "Who do y'all think I am?"

¹⁶ Pete spoke right up and said, "You are the cowboy we've been waiting on. You're the Boss' Son."

¹⁷ Jesus told him, "Pete, you will be granted favor for your answer. You didn't figure that out on your own. It was shown to you by the Boss. ¹⁸ I'm gonna call you Peter from now on. That means 'rock.' This truth that you have been shown is what I will build my ranch on and death itself won't be able to knock down its gates. ¹⁹ I'm gonna give you the key to the gates on this ranch and the Boss will allow on his place whatever you allow outside it. He won't allow anything inside that you don't allow outside."

²⁰ Jesus told all of them not to tell anyone that he was the cowboy that everyone had been lookin' for.

Jesus Tells Them He is Going to Die

²¹ From this point on, Jesus told his cowboys what was gonna happen to him. He said, "Pretty soon, I'm gonna ride up to Jerusalem and all those folks I've warned you about are gonna do some very terrible things to me. In the end, they're gonna string me up. But after three days, I will come back to life."

²² Pete took Jesus a little ways away and said, "The Boss ain't gonna let that happen so you need to quit talkin' nonsense!"

²³ Jesus turned on him and said, "Get away from me Devil! You're standin' in the way because you're acting like everyone else and not like the Boss wants you to."

²⁴ Then Jesus said to all the cowboys, "If y'all want to continue on in this crew, you need to forget about what you want and start focusin' on what the Boss wants. ²⁵ You gotta be willin' to give up your life and ride with me. ²⁶ What will you get if you gain everything

---

In verses 13-16, the apostles said that most people thought Jesus was a very good hombre or even a prophet—but Peter said that Jesus was something much greater: the Son of the living God. Who is Jesus to you?

In verses 21-23, Jesus said he would suffer while he was following God's trail, and when Peter protested Jesus' suffering, Jesus said Peter was thinking like a man and not like God. Has someone told you not to follow God because it would be too difficult?

this world has to offer and you still lose your soul? What can a man swap that's worth his soul?

[27] "The Boss' Son will soon return with all his Dad's crew and reward everyone for the things they do. [28] I'm tellin' you now that some of you that are hunkered down here with me now won't die before you see me comin'."

Matthew 17

Jesus then took Pete, James, and John with him up on a mountain. [2] It was on this mountain that Jesus was changed completely. His face shone brighter than the noon-day sun and his clothing turned bright white. [3] All of a sudden, two great cowboys from the past (Moses and Elijah) stood there with them visitin' with Jesus.

[4] Pete told Jesus, "I wouldn't have missed this for the world! I'm gonna put up three tents—one for you, one for Moses, and one for Elijah."

[5] While Pete was still runnin' his mouth, a big bright cloud surrounded everyone. A voice from the cloud said, "This is my Boy and I sure enough love him and he makes me proud. Listen to every word he says!"

[6] When Pete, James, and John heard this, they fell flat on the ground and whimpered like weaned pups. [7] But Jesus reached down and helped them up and told them, "Don't be scared!" [8] When they stood up, Jesus was the only one standin' there.

[9] As they rode down the mountain, Jesus told them, "Don't say anything about this to anyone until I have been raised from the dead."

[10] They asked him, "Why do the religious teachers say that old cowboy Elijah must come back first?"

[11] Jesus said, "Sure enough, a cowboy like Elijah comes and will make all things new. [12] But here's the thing, a cowboy like Elijah has already come and they didn't even recognize him. They treated him sorry and they will do the same to me." [13] The cowboys realized that Jesus was talkin' about his buddy John the Baptist.

In verses 24-26 (back on page 36), Jesus said if a man tries to save his own life, he'll lose it, but if a man gives his life to God, he'll save it—because only God can grant eternal life. Are you still trying to be your own pick-up man, or have you already saved your life by giving it to God?

In verses 14-21 (ahead on page 38), the disciples were not able to perform a miracle—perhaps, because they were trying to use their own power rather than the power of God. Have you been frustrated by trying to accomplish something by yourself when you should have turned it over to God?

Jesus Heals a Possessed Kid

¹⁴ They rode up to a crowd of people and a man came and knelt in the dirt before Jesus. ¹⁵ "Lord, please help my boy!" he said. "He has fits and suffers terribly. He falls into the fire and into the water trough. ¹⁶ I took him to some of your cowboys, but they couldn't help him."

¹⁷ Jesus said, "Good grief! Where is all of y'alls faith? How long am I gonna have to stick around and hold y'alls hand? I don't know how much more I can put up with. Bring that boy over here." ¹⁸ Jesus looked at the boy and told the demon that was possessing him to get out. From that moment, the boy was fine.

¹⁹ The cowboys asked Jesus, "How come we couldn't rope and drag that ol' demon out?"

²⁰ Jesus said, "Cause you don't have a squirt of faith. With a bit of faith, you could move mountains; anything is possible. (²¹ But this kind don't shuck loose without prayer and fasting.")

²² When all his cowboys had gathered with him near Galilee, he told 'em, "I'm gonna be double-crossed. ²³ They're gonna string me up, but on the third day after, I'm gonna be raised from the dead and brought back to life." The cowboys all looked down and some of them cried.

Pete and the Catfish

²⁴ When Jesus and his boys rode in Capernaum, a tax collector pulled Pete aside and asked if Jesus paid the church tax.

²⁵ "Of course he does!" Pete boasted.

When Pete caught up with the others, Jesus asked him, "Pete, do you think the governor of this territory or his family pays taxes for his salary or does he just make other people pay them?"

²⁶ "He don't pay taxes to himself. He just makes others pay them," Pete replied.

"Then his sons don't have to pay the taxes either," Jesus said. ²⁷ "I don't want to start any trouble here so I'll pay the tax that keeps my Father's house runnin' even though I don't have to. But I want you to go down to that pond and catch a fish. When you catch that catfish, open its mouth and there will be enough money for my tax and yours. Ride into town and pay it."

In verses 22-23, Jesus spoke about both his death and his comin' back to life, but the disciples acted like they only heard the bad news of his death so they were discouraged. Are you careful to always listen for the good news in the words of Christ?

In verses 24-26, Jesus provided the tax money for Peter, but Peter had to work to get it— which is an example of the way God gives us what we need, but he may want us to put in some effort. Do you believe all good things come from God, even though you work hard to get them?

Matthew 18

The Cowboys Argue Over Who is the Top Hand

The cowboys came up to Jesus and asked him, "Who is the top hand on the Boss' spread?"

[2] Jesus hollered for a little cowboy to come over there. He looked down at the small boy and [3] said, "Unless you can change and learn to have the same kind of faith and trust that this little cowboy does, you will never enter the Boss' ranch. [4] A little cowpoke like this depends 100% on those that take care of him and that's what you must do.

[5] "When you welcome a little child into your presence, you welcome me. [6] But I don't care who you are, if you make one of these kiddos their faith or their trust and cause them to sin, it would be better if you were killed by a pack of coyotes.

Jesus Warns Against Temptation

[7] "This whole world is headin' straight for a cliff because of their sins. It's sure enough gonna happen, but I feel sorry for the man that causes one of my little cowboys to sin. [8] If something is causin' you to sin, you better get rid of it. I don't care if it means you have to cut off one of your hands or shoot your best horse, it's better to have eternal life without a hand and a horse than to ride straight to hell with both hands. [9] If you can't even control your own eyes from causin' you to do things that the Boss wouldn't approve of, you best get a spoon and gouge 'em out. It's better for you to work for the Boss blind than to see the cliff that you are headed for and the hell that awaits you.

Do Not Be Uppity

[10] "Don't look down your nose at someone who has faith and trusts in me like a little child. [11] You probably don't realize that these people have winged riders that look upon the face of the Boss every day.

[12] "Let me ask you this. If you had a hundred cows, but one of them was missing, wouldn't you go look for it? [13] Wouldn't you be happy when you came over the hill and

---

In verses 1-3, Jesus said that the disciples must become like little kids to enter the kingdom of heaven—meaning they must become humble and realize they are dependent on God. Are you willing to admit you are weak like a child before God?

In verses 7-14, Jesus said there will be severe punishment for adults who lead children away from him, whether by exposing them to temptations or making them feel discouraged by looking down on them. Have you set a godly example for your children to follow?

39

saw it standing at the bottom? On the Boss' place, finding the one that wandered off is what is important. [14] He don't want a single one lost.

How to Handle Conflict with other Cowboys

[15] "If a cowboy that works for me does something to you that is against one of my rules (not yours), be a man and go talk to him about it. Let it be just between the two of you. Don't go round up all your buddies or even tell them what you're doin'. If he listens to you, y'all will be able to ride together. [16] If he won't listen to you, go ahead and take another cowboy along so that neither side will be able to accuse the other of something that was said. [17] If he still refuses to listen, take it to the men leadin' your crew. If he even refuses to listen to the cowboys I have chosen to be in charge of my outfit, just run him off. Treat him like you would a trespasser and get him off my place.

[18] "Whatever that crew decides is what will happen. The Boss will back them up!!

[19] "I'm tellin' you the truth. If two of my cowboys truly seek my guidance and my way, whatever they decide on will be backed up by me. [20] When two or more come to the campfire or anywhere else to be with me, I am there with them.

The Unforgiving Banker

[21] Then Pete came up to Jesus and asked, "If a cowboy just keeps doing me wrong, how many times do I have to let it go? Seven times?"

[22] Jesus replied, "No Pete, not seven times—every time!

[23] "The Boss' place is like a rancher who had loaned money to some of his cowboys. [24] He wanted to settle up the accounts before winter came on and he talked to a cowboy that owed him ten thousand dollars. [25] The cowboy wasn't able to pay the money so the rancher told his foreman to go and get every horse he owned, his horse trailer, his saddle, and his truck and sell all of them so he could get his money back.

[26] "The cowboy got down on his knees and begged the rancher not to take everything he owned and told him that he would repay every dollar. [27] The rancher felt kind of sorry for the cowboy and decided to cancel the whole debt.

[28] "When the cowboy left the headquarters, he ran into a fellow that owed him a hundred dollars. He reached out and grabbed the fellow by the throat and told him he had better pay him his hundred dollars.

In verse 15, Jesus said that if someone wrongs you, you should talk it over with him—the opposite of shunning him, which is what people usually do. The next time someone does you dirty, will you try to get revenge or will you reach out to them to talk?

In verses 23-25, Jesus pointed out that God has forgiven you for what you've done wrong, so you should forgive others for what they've done wrong. Is there someone that has wronged you that you have not forgiven?

[29] "The guy told him that he didn't have the money right then, but that he would pay back every cent.

[30] "But the cowboy would have none of it. He went and took the only horse the man had and sold it for a hundred dollars. [31] Some other cowboys saw all of this and they went and told the rancher what had happened.

[32] "The rancher called the cowboy in that had all his debt cancelled and said, 'You are one sorry son-of-a-gun!! I cancelled your whole debt of ten thousand dollars even though you had plenty of horses of your own and even a truck and a brand new trailer. [33] Then you went out and took a man's only horse from him because he owed you a hundred?!' [34] The rancher then had the guy beaten until he could pay back every cent he owed the rancher."

[35] "This is how my Father will run things on his ranch for those that don't let things go when they themselves have been forgiven."

Matthew 19

When Jesus finished up talkin' with everyone, he left and went into the territory on the other side of the Jordan River. [2] Truckloads of people followed him there and he was willin' to help everyone that needed it.

[3] Some of the Religious-Know-It-Alls tried to corner him with some fancy talkin'. They asked, "Don't you think a man should be able to bust up his marriage for whatever reason he wants?"

[4] "Don't you remember," he replied, "that the Boss made man and woman and [5] said that whenever they get married, they become one. [6] So they ain't two people anymore, but rather one. Whatever the Boss brings together no man should separate."

[7] "Why then," they replied, "did Moses say that a man could fill out a piece of paper that busted up the wedlock and then he could send her packin'?"

[8] Jesus told 'em, "He said y'all could divorce because you are a foolish bunch of people, but that's not the way my Dad planned it. [9] I'm tellin' you, if any cowboy sends

---

In verses 4-6, the religious leaders asked Jesus about divorce, but Jesus answered by talking about the importance of marriage as a part of God's plan for men and women. If you are married, when trouble comes, will you keep your focus on the relationship and not on splittin' up for good?

his bride away for any reason besides cheatin' on him, and marries another gal, he has committed adultery."

¹⁰ The cowboys on his crew said, "Man, if that's the case, we all ought to stay bachelors!"

¹¹ Jesus replied, "Not every cowboy can live up to the Boss' standards on marriage. ¹² Some men have been made into steers by birth and some by the business end of a pocket knife. Other cowboys have not got hitched because of ridin' for me. If this is the case, then all should accept it."

Jesus Blesses the Cowboy Kids

¹³ Then all the little kiddos gathered around Jesus so he could pray for 'em. But as soon as they got close, Jesus' cowboys started tellin' 'em to stand back.

¹⁴ Jesus shushed his boys and said, "Y'all let these little cowboys and cowgirls come and sit with me. Don't ever keep a kid from me because heaven belongs to folks like these." ¹⁵ When he had shook hands with all the kids and blessed 'em, he rode off.

Jesus and the Rich Fellow

¹⁶ A fellow walked up to Jesus and said, "Hey amigo! What kind of good deeds do I have to do to get an eternal job on the Boss' place?"

¹⁷ "Why are you askin' me about good things?" Jesus replied. "There is only One that fits the word good. If you want an eternal place on the ranch, you must hold to all the commandments."

¹⁸ "Which ones in particular?" the fellow asked.

Jesus said, "Don't kill, don't fool around on your spouse, don't rob, don't lie about other folks, ¹⁹ respect your ma and pa, and take care of your neighbors better'n you take care of yourself."

²⁰ "I've done all of these," the rich fellow said. "Is there anything else?"

²¹ Jesus smiled and said, "If you want to get an eternal spot on the ranch, go and give everything you got to those that don't have anything. By givin' everything you have away here, you will receive much more in heaven. Then when you're done, come and ride with me."

In verses 11-12, Jesus said there are good reasons not to marry, including the freedom to devote more time to serving God. If you are single, which do you think about more: finding someone to marry or finding more ways to serve God?

²²When the rich fellow heard this, he hung his head and walked away unwillin' to do as Jesus asked.

²³Jesus told his cowboys, "It's tough for a rich man to get an eternal spot on the ranch. ²⁴It's probably easier for a bull to give birth to a coyote than a rich man to enter the Forever Pastures."

²⁵This spooked the cowboys and they asked, "Who can get in then?"

²⁶Jesus looked at 'em and said, "Cowboys can't get themselves in, that would be impossible. But with God, all things are possible."

²⁷Pete said, "We've left everything behind and saddled up with you. What is that gonna get us?"

²⁸Jesus said, "I'm tellin' you, when all things are made new again and I sit on top of the hill on my Daddy's ranch, you cowboys that have followed me will sit on the twelve hills around me and judge the twelve territories of Israel. ²⁹And every cowboy or cowgirl who has left their own ranch, or their families, or kids or fields for me will receive a hundred times as much as they left and receive eternal life. ³⁰But many of the first to ride with me will be the last to come through the gate, and many who are the last to ride with me will be the first ones through the gate."

Matthew 20

"The Boss' ranch in heaven is like a ranch owner that went to the feed store early in the morning to hire some day workers to help with brandin' that day. ²He agreed to pay them one hundred dollars for their work that day.

³"About 9:00 a.m., he went out and saw some other cowboys hanging around the livery stables and not doin' anything. ⁴He told 'em, 'Y'all head out to my ranch and help with the brandin' and I'll pay you what is right for your time.' ⁵They saddled up and went.

"He rode out again at noon and then about three o'clock to look for more cowboys. ⁶At about five he rode by the saloon and found some cowboys just sittin' there playin'

In verse 23, Jesus said it is hard for a rich man to get into heaven, which showed that worldly riches are not always a sign of God's favor. Other than money, what are some things that you consider to be God lookin' out for you?

cards and drinkin' whiskey. The rancher asked them, 'Why have y'all just been sittin' around here not doin' anything all day long?'

⁷ 'Because no one gave us a job today,' they answered.

"He said to them, 'Y'all ride out to the ranch and help them with the brandin'.'

⁸ "When the sun went down that night, the ranch owner called his cattle foreman over to him and said, 'Call these cowboys over and I will pay them. Start with the last ones to ride up and end with the cowboys that have worked all day long in the sun and dirt.'

⁹ "The cowboys who had been playin' cards at the saloon and drinkin' whiskey all day walked over and the rancher paid them one hundred dollars. ¹⁰ When the cowboys who had been there since the sun came up walked over to get their wages, they assumed they would get much more, but they too were given one hundred dollars. ¹¹ When they saw that they had received the same amount for workin' all day as the last cowboys got for workin' an hour, they began to grumble and cuss about the rancher. ¹² 'These cowboys came up and only worked for an hour and barely broke one bead of sweat. You've paid them the same amount as us who've worked all day long in the heat, the sun, and the dirt!'

¹³ "But the rancher said to one of them, 'Cowboy, I ain't cheatin' you out of anything. You agreed to work for me today for one hundred dollars and that's what I paid you. ¹⁴ Take your wages and ride on out of here. I want to give every single cowboy that worked for me today one hundred dollars, regardless of how long they worked. ¹⁵ It is my money isn't it? I can spend my money however I want. Or do I need to ask you how to spend it? Are you bein' jealous just because I am generous?'

¹⁶ "The last to ride with me will be the first to enter the gate and the first will enter last."

Jesus Talks about Dying

¹⁷ As Jesus was ridin' up towards Jerusalem, he took the twelve cowboys that rode with him to the side and said, ¹⁸ "We are fixin' to get to Jerusalem and the Boss' Son will be double crossed by one of his own crew and handed over to the Hypocritical Preachers and Legalistic Teachers. They are going to sentence him to be strung up ¹⁹ and let those who aren't cowboys beat him and make fun of him and then kill him. On the third day though, he will be brought back from the dead and live!"

In verses 1-16, Jesus told a story to point out that anyone that accepts Christ as their Savior will get into heaven—whether they have followed him all their life or committed to him on their death bed. Have you thought that God liked lifelong Christians more than new Christians?

Serving Others

[20] Then James and John's momma came up to Jesus and kneeled down before him because she thought this might get her what she was fixin' to ask for.

[21] "What is it you're aimin' to get from me?" Jesus asked.

She said, "When you get control over the Boss' ranch in heaven, I'm askin' that my two boys ride with you and receive special treatment. I want one on the left and one on the right side of you."

[22] Jesus answered, "You don't know what you are asking for them. James and John, can you go through the pain and suffering that I am going to endure when they beat me and string me up?"

"We can," they told him.

[23] Jesus said, "You will go through some of the same suffering I will, but to ride at my left and right for eternity is not for me to decide. These positions of authority on the Boss' ranch are given by the Boss himself, not granted as favors."

[24] When the other ten cowboys heard what James and John were tryin' to get, they got ticked off. [25] Jesus called all of them over to him and said, "You know that the governors over the city folk (Gentiles) hold it over their people's heads that they have authority and power. [26] This ain't the way it works with y'all. If any of you want to become a top hand, you must serve and help the other cowboys, not tell them what to do. [27] A top hand is a slave to all the others. [28] The Boss' only Son did not come to tell other cowboys what to do, but to serve them and help them. He came to trade places with y'all and become the Outlaw's hostage to be killed so that y'all and every other person may be set free and live."

The Healing of the Blind

[29] When Jesus and his crew were riding away from Jericho, a bunch of people followed them. [30] Two blind men were sittin' by the road, and when they heard that it was the Boss' Son that was ridin' by they yelled, "Son of the Boss!! Have mercy on us!"

[31] All the people that followed Jesus yelled at the two blind men and told them to shut-up and be quiet, but the men shouted even louder, "Lord, have mercy on us!"

[32] Jesus pulled his horse to a stop and said, "What can I do for you?"

In verse 20, the mother of James and John seemed to worship Jesus so she could get him to do a favor—rather than worshiping Jesus for who he was, she worshiped him for what he could do for her. Do you follow Jesus for what he can do for you or what you can do for him?

In verses 24-28, Jesus said that while some people get ahead in the world by using others, the way to get ahead in the kingdom of God is by serving others. Would you rather get ahead in the world of men by being served or get ahead in the kingdom of God by being a servant?

³³ "We want to be able to see!" the two men said.

³⁴ Jesus felt sorry for them and climbed down off his horse and touched their eyes. Immediately they got their sight and they got up and followed him.

Matthew 21

Jesus Rides a Burro into Jerusalem

When they got close to Jerusalem, ² he told two of his cowboys, "Go into the village ahead and you will find a burro tied there with her colt standin' next to her. Untie them and bring them to me. ³ If anyone says anything, tell 'em that the Boss' Son needs them."

⁴ This happened to fulfill what had been said long ago:

> ⁵ *'Say to the daughter of Jerusalem, 'Look! Your king comes to you, gentle and ridin' on a donkey, not just any donkey, but the colt of a donkey.'*

⁶ The cowboys went into the village and did just what Jesus told 'em to. ⁷ They brought out the donkey and her colt, and used their jackets as a saddle blanket for the colt and Jesus got on. ⁸ A large crowd spread their ponchos, coats, and vests on the road and others cut branches off the trees and covered the ground with them. ⁹ The crowd of people went ahead of him and shouted,

"Yippe-ti-yi-yay, the Boss' Son has come!"

"Great is he who comes from the Lord!"

"Yippe-ti-yi-yo, the Boss' Son has come!"

¹⁰ When Jesus rode into Jerusalem, the whole town was askin', "Who is this cowboy?"

¹¹ The crowds shouted back, "This is Jesus, the Boss' Son from Nazareth in Galilee."

In verses 8-9, a large crowd of people said Jesus was Lord, but just a few days later, those same people would turn their backs and shuck out on him. If you have said that Jesus is your Lord, why would you ever turn your back on him?

Jesus Throws People out of the Church Building

¹² Jesus walked into the church building and started running everyone out that was buying and selling things. He knocked over the money changer's tables and the chairs of those that were selling doves for sacrifices. ¹³ "It was written long ago," Jesus said, "'My house will be a place where you could talk to me', but you have made it a 'den of thieves.'"

¹⁴ The blind and the crippled came to Jesus and he healed them all. ¹⁵ But when the uppity preachers and the my-way-or-the-highway teachers saw all the great things Jesus was doing and heard the little children shouting, "Yippe-ti-yi-yay to the Boss' Son!" they were mad.

¹⁶ "Do you hear what these kids are shouting?" they asked him.

"You bet I do!" Jesus said. "Have you never read, 'The little cowboys and cowgirls will sing songs of worship?'"

¹⁷ He then left the church and rode out to the small town of Bethany and spent the night there.

Jesus Curses the Fig Tree

¹⁸ The next morning as he was ridin' back to Jerusalem, Jesus wanted somethin' to eat because he was hungry. ¹⁹ He saw a fruit tree on the side of the trail and he rode up to it so he could get a piece of fruit, but all he found was leaves. Then he said to the tree, "You look good from a distance, but when I get close to you, I see you don't have any fruit. Because you haven't done what you were made to do, you will never be able to make fruit again!" Just then, the tree withered and died.

²⁰ When the cowboys saw this, they were astonished. "How come that tree withered and died right before our eyes?" they asked Jesus.

²¹ Jesus said, "Listen up and I'll tell you the truth. If you have faith and don't doubt one little bit, not only can you do what I did to this tree, but you could even tell the Rocky Mountains to go jump in the sea and they will do it. ²² If you believe, you will receive what you ask for when you talk to me in prayer."

The Authority of Jesus Is Questioned

²³ Jesus went into the church and started teachin'. The uppity preachers and some

In verses 12-13, Jesus drove the money changers out of the temple because they were cheating people and blocking the place of worship. Have you ever got mad at someone or a situation 'cause you knew that God wouldn't like it either?

In verse 19-22, Jesus cursed a fig tree that did not show any fruit to make a point about people who appear to be ridin' for him but don't do anybody any good. Do you know someone who talks about ridin' for the Lord but hardly ever toes a stirrup?

old coots came up to him and asked him, "Who told you that you could do these things? And who gave you the authority to do them?"

²⁴ Jesus told 'em, "First, let me ask you a question. If you can answer mine, I will answer yours. ²⁵ John's baptism, where did it come from? Was it from the Boss or from men?"

They talked about it and finally said among themselves, "If we say that it came from the Boss, then he will say, 'Then how come you didn't believe John?' ²⁶ If we tell him it came from man, then all these cowboys are going to get mad and throw us out because they think he came on the Boss' word."

²⁷ They finally just threw their hands up and said, "We don't know."

Then Jesus said, "Since you didn't answer, neither will I."

The Good Son and the Bad Son

²⁸ Jesus said, "Let me ask y'all this. There was a cowboy that had two boys. He went to the oldest and said, 'Go check on the cattle in the pasture and make sure they are all there.'

²⁹ "'I'm not goin' to check on anything,' the boy said, but later he felt bad and went and checked on the cattle.

³⁰ "Then the cowboy went and told the second boy to do the same thing and go check on the cattle. The boy said, 'Yes sir! I'll go right now,' but the boy never did.

³¹ "Which of the two boys did what their dad wanted them to?"

"The first boy," they said.

Jesus told 'em, "Listen to what I say, the bank robbers and the hookers are getting to the Boss' ranch in heaven before you are! ³² John came and showed you how to make things right with the Boss and you shunned his message, but the bank robbers and hookers listened to him. Even after all you have seen, you still don't turn from your sorry way of life or believe him.

³³ "Listen to this story: There was a farmer who planted a field of alfalfa. He fenced it off and even put a lookout tower on the edge of the field. After all the work was done, he rented it out to some other people and went on a long adventure. ³⁴ When it was time for the hay to be baled, the farmer sent some of his employees to collect his part of the hay.

[35] "The renters took the employees and beat the snot out of one of 'em and killed two of the others. [36] The farmer then sent some more hired hands and the renters jumped them and did the same thing they had before. [37] Finally, the farmer sent his only son. He thought surely they would respect him.

[38] "The renters saw the son comin' and said to one another, 'Here comes the farmer's boy! If we kill him, then we can have his inheritance and own this place.' [39] So they took the son and strung him up.

[40] "What do y'all think the farmer is gonna do to these renters?" Jesus asked.

[41] "The farmer is gonna kill them all and take back the field and rent it to some people that will bale the hay like they are supposed to and give the farmer his part," they replied.

[42] Jesus said to them, "Have you never read the Good Book where it says:

> *'The perfect Calf has been rejected by the cowboys. The Lord has done this and it's amazin' to our eyes.'*

[43] "The Boss' ranch is going to be taken from the cowboys he entrusted it to and given to those who will work the ranch and give back to him what he is due. [44] The cowboy that ignores this Calf and falls over it will be broken, but the cowboy on whom the Calf steps will be crushed."

[45] When the uppity preachers and the Religous-Know-It-Alls heard this story, they knew that Jesus was talkin' about them. [46] They wanted a reason to throw him in jail, but they were afraid because the people thought he was sent from God.

Matthew 22

The Wedding BBQ

Jesus told another story and said, [2] "The Boss' place is like a big rancher who planned a BBQ for his son's wedding. [3] He sent some of his cowboys to the other ranches to invite them to the BBQ, but no one came.

In verses 1-5, Jesus told a story about a king who invited people to a party more than one time, but the people ignored his invites. Do you know people who keep ignoring God's invitations to ride with him—or are you one of 'em?

⁴ "Then he sent some more cowboys to the neighbors he had invited with the message: 'I've butchered my best steer and the fattest hogs. Y'all be sure and put your cowboy hats on. That's the only thing I ask. Come get the best food in the world and help celebrate my son's wedding.'

⁵ "But nobody came and they all ignored the invitation. They were too busy for the big rancher. One went and worked his new colt, and another went ropin'. ⁶ The other folks that were invited were just bored so they beat up the big rancher's cowboys and even killed a few of them. ⁷ The big rancher was furious! He sent his hired guns to kill those that had murdered his cowboys and they even burned their ranches to the ground.

⁸ "Then he said to his cowboys, 'The wedding BBQ is ready, but no cowboys wanted to come. ⁹ Go into the city and invite anyone you find. Tell them to put their hats on and come help me celebrate.' ¹⁰ The cowboys went into to the city and invited everyone they saw. It didn't matter if they were good or bad. They invited everyone, and the ranch headquarters was packed with people.

¹¹ "But when the big rancher came out of the house, he saw a guy standin' over to one side and he wasn't wearin' a hat. ¹² 'Hey friend,' he said, 'how did you get through the gate without a hat on? That was the only requirement to attend.' The man stood there speechless.

¹³ "The big rancher told some of his cowboys, 'Tie him up and drag him out of here and leave him for the coyotes and buzzards to eat!'

¹⁴ "Many will be invited, but only a few will come."

Taxes

¹⁵ Then the Religous-Know-It-Alls tried to trap Jesus with his own words so they could arrest him. ¹⁶ They sent some people to ask him, "We know you're a great cowboy and good teacher of what the Boss wants. You don't care what men think about you or what they say. ¹⁷ Since you don't care, is it right for us to pay taxes to Caesar?"

¹⁸ Jesus knew they were tryin' to trap him with their words and he said, "Why are you dealin' words off the bottom of the deck and tryin' to trap me with the dead man's hand of aces and eights? ¹⁹ Show me a dollar that you would pay your taxes with." They showed him a silver dollar, ²⁰ and he asked, "Whose picture is stamped on this dollar?"

In verses 11-14, Jesus continued the story, saying that one cowboy at the party did not act the right way—meaning he refused to do what he was supposed to in order to join in the celebration. When God invites you into his kingdom, will you make sure you are ready ride the right way?

²¹ "That's Caesar's picture," they said.

Then he told 'em, "If it has his picture on it, then give it back to him. Give to Caesar what belongs to Caesar and give to the Boss what belongs to the Boss."

²² They didn't know what to say to this so they just left.

Being Hitched in Heaven

²³ The Cattle Barons (Sadducees), who were a group of influential people who didn't believe in life after death, came to Jesus and said, ²⁴ "Moses said that if a man dies without having any kids, the dead cowboy's brother needs to marry his brother's wife, and if they have a son, the son will be considered the dead brother's son.²⁵ If there were seven brothers and the first one married a gal and died before having a child, and then the ²⁶ second brother married her and the same thing happened, and it went on until the seventh brother married her ²⁷ and she died, ²⁸ who would be married to her in heaven since she was married to all of 'em?"

²⁹ Jesus answered, "Y'all don't know scripture from scribblin'! And you don't know who God is. ³⁰ When God opens the gates of heaven for those that believe in his boy, they won't be hitched to nobody. They'll be like the winged riders that serve him. ³¹ As far as being given eternal life, the Boss was talkin' at you when he said, ³² 'I'm the Boss of Abraham, the first ramrod of my outfit, and of all his sons.' My Dad isn't the Boss of the dead, but of those who are alive!"

³³ The cowboys and cowgirls gathered there stood with their mouths hanging open in surprise at what Jesus was teachin'.

The Greatest Task

³⁴ After Jesus had made the Cattle Barons look like a bunch of idiots, the Hypocritical Preachers got together to talk about what he was sayin'. ³⁵ One of them was a know-it-all when it came to the Code of Moses and he tried to trap Jesus with a question. He asked Jesus, ³⁶ "What's the most important task in the Code of Moses?"

³⁷ Jesus said, "Love the Boss with everything you got and everything you are. ³⁸ This is the first task and it's the most important. ³⁹ The second most important is to love other cowboys and cowgirls as you love yourself. ⁴⁰ Everything in the Code and the writings of the Boss' Cowboys (prophets) are based on these two tasks."

In verses 34-40, Jesus said that all of the Ten Commandments can be followed by obeying the two most important commandments—love God and love your neighbor as you love yourself. In your daily life, are you obeying the two most important commandments?

The Son of David

⁴¹ While the Hypocritical Preachers were still standin' there, Jesus asked them, ⁴² "What do y'all think about the One Who Will Save All Cowboys? Where will he come from?" They looked at each other and said, "He will be a son of David."

⁴³ Jesus then asked, "Alright then, if this Savin' Cowboy is David's son, then why did David say this Cowboy would be his Master? Remember David said, ⁴⁴ 'The Boss said to my Master: Ride here beside me until I make all your enemies into something that you can rest and prop your boots on.'"

⁴⁵ "If David called this Cowboy his Master, how can this Cowboy be a son of King David?" ⁴⁶ No one knew the answer and from that day on, everyone kept their mouths shut and didn't try to trap him with fancy words.

Matthew 23

Jesus Puts Down Religious Nonsense

Jesus turned and talked to his cowboys and the rest of the folks that were sittin' around. He said, ² "The Hypocritical Preachers and the Lawyers of the Code are experts in the Law of Moses. ³ Y'all need to do what they say, but don't act like they act. They sure as heck don't practice what they preach.

⁴ "They will load y'all down with impossible tasks that they wouldn't be willing to bear. ⁵ They have silver on their saddles and jingle bobs on their spurs, just so y'all will think they are important. They are all talk and no action. ⁶ They like the box seats at the rodeo and want to be the first in line at the chuckwagon. ⁷ They care about bein' recognized at the feed store and bein' called by fancy titles.

⁸ "But y'all cowboys that ride for me don't need fancy titles. Y'all have only one Boss and you are all brothers. ⁹ Don't call anyone on earth 'boss' because you only have one Boss and he is in heaven. ¹⁰ Don't let anyone call you 'teacher' either. You only have one Teacher and he's the Boss' Son. ¹¹ The one that is the top hand among you will be your servant that works like a pack mule. ¹² Whoever tries to rise above others will be thrown down and whoever lowers himself will be raised up.

In verse 11, Jesus said the greatest person is a servant—meaning you should focus on helping other people instead of always trying to benefit yourself. The last time you talked to someone else, were you trying to help them or yourself?

In verse 12, Jesus said that the person who is puffed up like a banty rooster is in for a fall, but the person who is humble will find God's approving nod. Based on your attitude lately, do you think you deserve a fall or the nod of his head?

Jesus Gives it to the Religous-Know-It-Alls

[13] "You Hypocritical Preachers and Lawyers of the Code are going to come to a terrible reckonin'. [14] You slam the gate to God's Green Pastures in the face of cowboys and cowgirls. Y'all won't ever ride through those gates, nor will you allow anyone else to ride through.

[15] "You Hypocritical Preachers and Lawyers of the Code are going to come to a terrible reckonin'. You ride over mountains and cross great territories to win one cowboy for the Boss, and when he saddles up, you make him twice the son of hell that you are.

[16] "You blind trail guides have a day of reckonin' comin' to you too! You tell folks, 'If you give your word by the church building, it don't mean nothin'; but if you give your word by the gold in the church, you are obligated to keep it.' [17-19] You blind idiots! Which is more important: the gift, or the means by which the gift is made? [20-21] Those who give their word by the church do it by the church and everything it stands for. [22] The cowboy that gives his word by heaven gives his word on the Boss' throne and by the one who sits on it.

[23] "You Hypocritical Preachers and Lawyers of the Code are going to come to a terrible reckonin'. Y'all give a tenth of everything from tobacco to toilet paper, but you forget about the important part of the Code: mercy, justice, and faith. You should give a tenth of everything, but don't forget the more important matters. [24] You blind trail guides will pick a piece of dirt out of your coffee, but then eat a mud pie.

[25] "You Hypocritical Preachers and Lawyers of the Code are going to come to a terrible reckonin'. You'll wash the dirt off the outside of your coffee cup, but leave the inside full of greed and perversion. [26] If you'll get the inside clean the outside will follow!

[27] "You Hypocritical Preachers and Lawyers of the Code are going to come to a terrible reckonin'. You are like pretty cedar caskets. You look good on the outside, but on the inside you are full of rotting flesh and worms. [28] That's the way y'all appear to people. You look good on the outside, but inside you are full of hypocrisy and rebellion.

[29] "You Hypocritical Preachers and Lawyers of the Code are going to come to a terrible reckonin'. You carve fancy headstones for the prophets and decorate the graves of those who rode with the Boss. [30] You say, 'If we lived way back then, we

wouldn't have been a part of the posse that murdered these great people!' [31] But you are proof that you are the sons of those posse riders. [32] Just keep on doin' the same things they did and actin' the way they acted. [33] You're all coyotes! You're the bastard sons of coyotes! How are you gonna escape the truck that leads to the slaughter house? [34] I will send my cowboys and wise foremen and experts in the Code of Moses to you. But y'all will string 'em up or nail 'em to a cross or whip 'em away from your meetings or run 'em out of town. [35] That's why you'll be found guilty for every cowboy, starting with Abel. [36] I promise that you people livin' today will be punished for all these things.

Jesus Cries about Jerusalem Again

[37] "Oh my town of Jerusalem! You have killed all those I sent to take care of you. I want so bad to take all your children and comfort them like a momma hen comforts her chicks, but you have shunned me. [38] Now your church will be deserted and full of tumbleweeds. [39] You ain't gonna see me again until you say, 'Blessed is the cowboy that comes in the name of the Boss.'"

Matthew 24

The Church Building and the Return of Jesus

After Jesus left the church, his cowboys were all gawkin' and talkin' about how big everything was. [2] Jesus told 'em, "All this stuff, no matter how big or how nice it is, will be torn down. There won't be one brick that stays where it's at."

[3] Later, Jesus was backed up against a tree resting on top of Olive Hill. A few of his cowboys came up and asked, "How will we know when you're ridin' back to get us? Are you gonna give us a whistle or a yell or send us a telegram?"

[4] Jesus thought hard and then his eyebrows knitted together as he spoke. "Don't let anyone pull the wool over your eyes. [5] There's gonna be a whole mess of people that claim to be me. They will ride into town and claim to be the Cowboy that has come to save them.

[6] You will hear about wars and battles, but don't fret, this isn't the end. These things must happen, but it ain't the end. [7] Nations and countries will kill each other. Folks will

---

In verse 37, Jesus said he wanted to ride shotgun for his people but his people would not let him—even in times of trouble, they refused to turn to him for help. Have you failed to ask God for help when you've been bucked off in life because you thought he could not provide what you need?

In verse 3, the disciples asked Jesus when he will come ridin' back again—but instead of answering that question, Jesus told them how to be ready for that day. If today was the day that Jesus rode back, would you be ready to stand tall before him?

starve to death in their own houses and there will be earthquakes in many different territories. [8] But this is just the birthin' of the problems that will follow.

[9] "Y'all are gonna be beaten and even killed. They will hate you because you ride for me. [10] Folks are gonna start stabbin' each other in the back every day. [11] And a lot of snake-oil salesmen will come and lead many people down the wrong trail. [12] Folks are gonna stop lovin' each other and focus on themselves and the evil that lives there. [13] But if y'all keep your hearts on my message and keep ridin' for me all day, every day, you will be spared and saved. [14] When the good news of my tale has finally been taken to every part of every territory, then the end will come.

The Defecation of Desecration

[15] "One day you will see the most horrible thing in the world. You will see the 'Defecation of Desecration' right there in the church's most holy place. If you've read what Daniel wrote you'll know what I mean when I say that everyone should try real hard to understand. [16] If you're livin' in or around Judea when this happens, saddle up your horse right then, not later, and shuck out for the hills. [17] If you're patchin' some shakes on the roof, don't even go back inside, just ride. [18] If you're muckin' out stalls, don't go back in and change boots. [19] This ride will be double tough on pregnant womenfolk and those with babies that are still on the suck. [20] You ought to pray that this time don't come in the winter or on Sunday, when you're supposed to be restin'. [21] This time is gonna be plum awful. Nothin' like this has ever been seen or will ever be seen again. [22] If the Boss don't step in with his mighty hand and make this time as short as possible, ain't nobody gonna make it out alive. Nobody! But because God loves the cowboys that ride for him, he's gonna step in and make sure it don't go on too long.

[23] "People may yell, 'Here's Jesus!!' or 'There he is, I see him!' but don't believe them. [24] Jesus impersonators and fake cowboys will come and do amazin' things and fool people. They will even try to fool those cowboys that ride for my father's brand. [25] I'm readyin' the trail for you and givin' you ample warning ahead of time. [26] If a city slicker tells you that Jesus is out in the desert, don't believe them. If someone tells you that I am in a hidden place and they know where to find me, don't believe their forked tongue. [27] When the Boss' Son returns, you'll know for sure. It'll be like the sky has been cracked open and lightning and thunder have come alive and rode straight from heaven itself. Every cowboy and every city slicker on earth will be able to see and hear it. [28] If you see a crowd of people gathered like buzzards and you don't know what they are lookin' at, it sure enough won't be me. Buzzards circle around the dead, not the Boss' Son.

In verses 12-13, Jesus said that during times of trouble, most people will turn away from God—but the people who sit tall in the saddle of their faith will be saved. During times of trouble or temptation in your ride through life's pastures, do you sit tall and ride with Jesus?

When the Son Arrives

²⁹ "After the Boss steps in and all the sufferin' is over,

'The sun will go out and the moon won't shine anymore.
The stars will fall and every universe will tremble.'

³⁰ "When this happens, the Son will ride back. Every person will see it and there will be NO doubt. People that have chosen to ride alone or with someone else, instead of with me, will cry and wail in terror when they see me ride out of heaven with all the power of God in my right hand. ³¹ At the sound of the bugler's charge, the Son will send all the winged riders to gather all the earth, the faithful that have chosen to ride with him.

³² "Learn a lesson from a fruit tree. When the branches start buddin' out, you know warmer weather is approachin'. ³³ When you see all these things I told you start happenin', you'll know that I am approachin'. ³⁴ I ain't just talkin' to people hundreds of years from now, I'm talkin' right at y'all sitting here too. ³⁵ The rocks imbedded in the deepest mountains and the blue sky over your heads will not last forever, but my word will.

³⁶ "Nobody but the Boss knows the day or the hour all of this will happen. The winged riders don't know. Your know-it-all neighbor don't know. Not even the Boss' Son knows. Only the Boss knows. ³⁷ When you see the Boss' Son come back, it will be just like when the rain started fallin' in the time of Noah. ³⁸ Folks were cookin' on the grill and havin' their drink of choice and celebratin' weddings right up to the time that Noah jumped on the big boat. ³⁹ Despite everythin' that Noah told 'em, they were surprised when the flood came and washed 'em down the gulley. This is exactly how it will be when I come back.

⁴⁰ Two cowboys will be gatherin' cattle and one will be taken and the other left right there in the saddle. ⁴¹ Two cowgirls will be feedin' horses and one will be taken and the other left standin' right there. ⁴² Be on the lookout and don't get lax in the saddle. Keep both feet in your stirrups and one eye on the sky. You won't know when I'm comin' back, so be ready. ⁴³ You got to keep a sharp watch. If you knew what time a horse thief was comin', you would be ready with your rifle. ⁴⁴ Mark my words and be ready for the Son to come ridin' back down.

⁴⁵ "Who are the top-hands and faithful riders of the brand? Who will the Boss choose to make foreman and ramrods? ⁴⁶ Cowboys that are found doin' their job when the

---

In verses 45-47, Jesus told the disciples how to spend their time until he comes again—by helping others as servants of God. In the pastures you ride, who are some of the people you could help serve?

cattle foreman shows up unannounced will be rewarded. [47] If a cowboy does his job the way it's supposed to be done, then he will be promoted on the Boss' spread. [48] But what about the cowboy out there in that far line camp that thinks nobody is watchin'? [49] Suppose he quits checkin' the waters and fails to feed cow-cake in the winter. What if he invites all his buddies out to the house and all they do is get drunk and pitch washers instead of what he's supposed to be doing? [50] You can bet that one day the cattle foreman will ride up to the camp without givin' any notice. [51] This cowboy will be thrown off the ranch along with the all the others that pretend to ride for the brand. There they will be exposed to pain and sufferin' like nobody has ever seen.

Matthew 25

The Ten Single Gals

"God's Green Pasture is like what happened one night when ten single gals went to meet a famous cowboy. [2] They all took kerosene lanterns because they knew he would be arriving very late. Five of the girls were smart and five of the girls were dumb. [3] The dumb ones took their lanterns, but didn't take any extra oil. [4] The smart ones were prepared for the whole night.

[5] "The cowboy was comin' from another ranch and would arrive very late. They waited on him all that night to be the first to welcome him. [6] In the middle of the night, someone shouted, 'The cowboy is here! Come and say hello.'

[7] "The girls got up and all had left their lanterns burning. [8] The dumb girls said to the others, 'Give us some of your oil. Our lanterns are going out and we won't be able to see.'

[9] "The smart cowgirls said, 'There ain't enough for all of us. You'll have to go buy some more.'

[10] "While the dumb girls were off buying more oil, the cowboy rode up. The girls with the lit lanterns walked with him to the house where he was stayin'. They went in to visit and the door was closed. [11] Later, the dumb girls got back and knocked on the door and said, 'We want to meet you. Can we come in?'

In verses 1-13, Jesus told a story about how each of us is responsible for his own spiritual life—because it cannot be borrowed or bought from someone else. Do you act like you're responsible for your spiritual life—or do you think just being in the company of Christians will be enough?

¹² "But the cowboy replied, 'I've never seen y'all before. The girls that wanted to meet me were waiting on me to get here.'

¹³ "I want y'all that ride with me to pay attention to this story and always be ready. You need to be prepared because you won't know when all this will happen.

The Three Cowboys and Their Talents

¹⁴ "The Boss' place is also like a rancher that went away and left three of his cowboys in charge of training the comin' two-year-old colts. ¹⁵ He knew what each cowboy was capable of so he gave the first cowboy five colts to break, the second cowboy three colts to break, and one colt to the third.

¹⁶ "As soon as the rancher was gone, the first cowboy broke all five of his colts and then swapped them for ten unbroken colts. ¹⁷ The cowboy with two colts did the same thing. ¹⁸ But the cowboy with one colt was afraid to even work with the horse. He locked it in a stall so nothing would go wrong and the horse would be safe. He didn't ride it or even halter break it.

¹⁹ "When the rancher returned, he asked them about the horses he had assigned them. ²⁰ The cowboy who got five horses told about how he had done some horse trading and showed him the ten saddle broke horses. The cowboy said, 'You gave me five horses that couldn't be ridden and now you have ten that you can.'

²¹ "'Great job,' the rancher said, 'I'm gonna make you a full partner on this outfit. I put you in charge of just a little bit, but now I will put you in charge of more. Get your stuff out of the bunkhouse and put it in the big house.'

²² "The cowboy who had been given the two colts walked with the rancher to another set of pens. The cowboy said, 'You gave me two horses that couldn't be ridden and now you have four that you can.'

²³ "'Great job,' the rancher said, 'I'm gonna make you a full partner on this outfit. I put you in charge of just a little bit, but now I will put you in charge of more. Get your stuff out of the bunkhouse and put it in the big house.'

²⁴ "The cowboy that had received one colt walked with the rancher over to the stall where he had kept the one horse. The cowboy said, 'I know you're a hard man and don't tolerate excuses or shoddy work. ²⁵ I was afraid that something might happen to this colt so I just kept him in here so he would be safe.'

In verses 14-28, Jesus told a story about how God has given each of us talents to use to spread his kingdom on earth. What are some of the ways you are using your abilities to spread God's kingdom?

58

²⁶ "The rancher was furious and said, 'You know that I'm a hard man and I don't tolerate excuses or shoddy work! ²⁷ You could have at least broke this horse so I could use him durin' brandin' season coming up.'

²⁸ "Then the rancher said, 'Take this colt and give it to the cowboy with the ten horses. ²⁹ Everyone who risks everything for me will be given more, but for those that are scared and cautious, all will be taken from them. ³⁰ I know city slickers that are better cowboys than you are. You are gonna be thrown off this ranch where you will suffer in great pain and cry all day and all night.'

The Sheep and the Goats

³¹ "When the Son comes back with all his winged riders and all the power of heaven with him, he will sit upon the highest peak of the ranch. ³² Every territory and every nation will be gathered below him and he will separate the sheep from the goats. ³³ He will put the sheep on his right side and the goats to the left.

³⁴ "Then the Lord of the ranch will say to those sheep on his right, 'Come, all you who are blessed by the Boss, inherit the ranch that was made for you at the beginning of all creation. ³⁵ I was hungry and you fed me. I was thirsty and you watered me. I was a stranger on a lonely road and you welcomed me into your home. ³⁶ I had no chaps to protect me and you gave some to me. I was sick and dyin' and you cared for me. I was locked up in jail and you came to visit me.'

³⁷ "Then these cowboys and cowgirls that had done right in the Lord's eyes will say, 'When did we ever see you like this? ³⁸ When did we give you a room or hand you a pair of batwing leggings? ³⁹ When did we visit you in the juzgow?'

⁴⁰ "And the Lord will say, 'I'm tellin' it to y'all straight. Every time you did these things for one of the cowboys or cowgirls that rode for my Father's brand, you did them for me too.'

⁴¹ "Then the Lord will turn to the goats on his left and say, 'Get these sorry mongrels off my spread! Put them on the killer trucks and ship them off to the fire that never goes out—the fire that was prepared for the devil and his demons! ⁴² I was hungry and you refused me food. I was thirsty and you laughed. ⁴³ I was a stranger in need and you ignored me. Thorns cut my legs and it made no difference to you. I was sick and in jail and you never visited me.'

⁴⁴ "Then they will cry out, 'Lord, we never saw you hungry, thirsty, or any of those

---

In verses 31-46, Jesus told a story about how we should treat others like we would treat Jesus—so whether they are hungry, thirsty, or lonely, we should help to take care of their needs. Are you helping those around you that are in need?

59

other things. If we would have seen you, we would have done something.'

⁴⁵ "And he will answer, 'Listen to me close. When you refused these things to the cowboys and cowgirls that rode for my Father's brand, you refused them to me!'

⁴⁶ "And then they will be shipped off to the fires of hell, but those cowboys and cowgirls that rode for the Father's brand will be turned out to lush, eternal pasture."

Matthew 26

Planning and Plotting to Kill Jesus

When Jesus was done talking, he said to his cowboys, ² "Passover is in a couple of days and it will be then that the Boss' Son will be double-crossed by one of his own and killed."

³ It was at this time that the big wigs of the church were meetin' at the high priest's townhouse and ⁴ tryin' to come up with a plan to kill Jesus. ⁵ "We can't do anything durin' the Passover," they agreed, "or we will have a riot on our hands."

Jesus at Bethany

⁶ Meanwhile, Jesus was hangin' out in the town of Bethany with a fellow named Simon that used to have the bad skin rot. ⁷ While he was there, a woman came in with a jar of very expensive perfume and she used all of it on Jesus.

⁸ The cowboys couldn't believe she had wasted something so valuable by just pourin' it on Jesus. ⁹ "That could have been sold for a bunch of money and given to those that can't buy food or clothes!" they said.

¹⁰ But Jesus got on to them and said, "Wait a minute! Why are y'all criticizin' what this cowgirl has done for me? ¹¹ There will always be poor folks, but I won't always be here like I am now. ¹² She has poured this perfume on me to prepare my body for the grave. ¹³ I'm tellin' you the truth when I say that this woman's deed here tonight will be remembered and taught wherever the Good News is preached throughout this entire world."

In verses 6-7, a woman used a jar of perfume to show Jesus she loved him—which was a hard thing for her to give up, because she was poor and the perfume was expensive. When you give something to God, do you only give what is easy to give up?

Judas Double-Crosses Jesus

¹⁴ About this time, the dirty double crosser Judas Iscariot, one of the cowboys that rode for Jesus, went to the leaders in the church ¹⁵ and asked, "How much will you pay me to double-cross Jesus?" They handed him thirty pieces of silver. ¹⁶ He then began lookin' for a way to ambush Jesus and turn him over to them.

The Last Supper

¹⁷ On the first day of the Celebration of the Thin Bread, the cowboys that rode for Jesus came up to him and asked, "Where are we supposed to make the biscuits for the Passover Supper?"

¹⁸ "When you get to town," Jesus said, "you will see a certain fellow. Tell him, 'The Top Hand says: My time is up and I will eat the Passover Supper at your table with the cowboys that ride for me.'" ¹⁹ The cowboys did what they were told to do and made sup' where they were told to.

²⁰ After the sun had gone down, Jesus sat down at the table with all of his cowboys. ²¹ While they were eatin' he said, "Y'all listen up! One of you is a dirty double-crosser and has betrayed me."

²² The cowboys couldn't believe their ears and each one asked, "It ain't me is it, Lord?"

²³ He replied, "One of you who is sittin' at this table sharin' biscuits with me is the dirty rat. ²⁴ The Boss' Son must die as it was said long ago in the Good Book. But it's gonna be awfully terrible for the one that snitches him off. It would have been better if he'd never been born."

²⁵ Judas, the one who would do the dirty deed, also asked, "Do you think it's me?"

Jesus told him, "You said it, I didn't."

²⁶ As they were eatin', Jesus took a biscuit and blessed it. Then he broke it into some pieces and handed a piece to each cowboy. He said, "Take this and eat it. It represents my body that will be broken for y'all and every other cowboy and cowgirl."

²⁷ Then Jesus took a coffee cup that had wine in it and blessed it. He passed it around the table for everyone to get a drink and said, "Y'all take a swig of this. ²⁸ It represents my blood that my Dad will use to make a new agreement with everyone that believes

In verses 14-16, Judas asked the religious leaders how much they would pay him to double-cross Jesus—because he was more focused on himself than God's kingdom. As you go about your day, what are you focused on?

in me. My blood will be spilt in the dirt as a sacrifice so that the sins of many will be forgiven. ²⁹ I won't drink wine again until the day I drink it with y'all on my Father's spread."

³⁰ They sang a song about God and went to Olive Hill.

Peter is Gonna Deny Jesus

³¹ As they rode over to Olive Hill, Jesus told them, "Tonight, all of y'all are gonna shuck out on me. The Good Book says,

'The Boss will slay the Trail Guide and the herd will scatter.'

³² But after I come back from the grave, I will meet ya'll in Galilee."

³³ Pete said, "I don't care if everyone shucks out for the hills, I ain't leavin' you."

³⁴ I'm tellin' you the truth, Pete," Jesus said. "Before the sun comes up, you will deny that you ever rode with me three times."

³⁵ Pete stood up and stomped his foot as he said, "Even if I have to die with you to prove it, I will never deny ridin' with you." And all of Jesus' crew made the same vow and waved their hats in the air.

Torture in the Garden

³⁶ Then Jesus and his boys rode over to a place called Gethsemane and he told 'em, "Y'all wait here while I go over yonder and talk to my Dad." ³⁷ He motioned for Pete, James, and John to go with him and Jesus began to get upset and troubled. ³⁸ Then Jesus told the three cowboys, "I feel as if I will be crushed by the pain and sorrow I'm feelin' right now. I'm worried that it might actually kill me. Y'all wait right here and take first watch while I go and talk to my Dad."

³⁹ Jesus rode a little further and then stepped off and laid face down in the dirt and said, "Daddy, please don't make me go through this cruel deed that is comin'. If it's possible, will you find another way? But if this is the only way and it is your will, then I'll do it."

⁴⁰ Jesus rode back over to where his boys were keepin' watch and found them fast asleep. "Could y'all not keep watch like I asked you to for even one hour?" he asked Pete. ⁴¹ "Say your prayers and keep watch so that you will not fall into temptation again.

In verse 35, all of the disciples said they would die before they would turn their backs on Jesus—but a few hours later, all of them scattered like quail when he was arrested. When someone insults Jesus or criticizes Christianity, do you turn away or stand up to that person?

I know that your hearts are willin' to ride with me no matter what, but your bodies are weaker'n pond water."

[42] Jesus went away a second time and prayed, "Daddy, if there ain't another way to get this done except by me going through this dastardly deed, then so be it. I just want to please you."

[43] When Jesus went back to his boys, he found them asleep again. [44] This time, he didn't say anything, but went back and prayed a third time, sayin' the exact same thing.

[45] He finally came back and woke them up by sayin' to them, "Are y'all still sleepin'? Get up, for the hour has come, and the Boss' Son has been double-crossed by one of his own cowboys into the hands of sinners. [46] Get up now! We will go meet them and not let them find us cowerin' in a garden. Here comes my betrayer now!"

Jesus is Double-Crossed and Arrested

[47] While Jesus was sayin' this, Judas, one of the twelve cowboys that rode with Jesus, arrived at the garden. Following Judas was a posse of armed men, sent from the big wigs of the church. [48] Judas told the posse to watch and he would give them a sign as to which man was Jesus. "The one I walk up and shake hands with is Jesus. He's the one to arrest." [49] Judas walked straight up to Jesus and said, "How ya doin', boss!!" and shook Jesus' hand.

[50] Jesus said, "Alright boys, y'all go ahead and do what you've come to do."

A few guys from the posse stepped forward and grabbed Jesus. [51] Right then, one of Jesus' cowboys pulled a knife out of his boot and cut off one of the man's ears that had grabbed him.

[52] "Put that knife away," Jesus said, "if you pull a knife you will die by the knife. [53] If I wanted to defend myself, I could ask my Father to send twelve thousand winged riders to come and rescue me. [54] But if I did this, how would the things that must be done be fulfilled?"

[55] Jesus turned to the posse and asked, "Am I the leader of some outlaw gang? Have I done any violence to anyone that warrants y'all comin' out here to arrest me with all these weapons? Every day I sat in the church teachin' everyone about God and you never arrested me there. [56] But all of this must happen this way in order to fulfill what the great cowboys that rode for my Dad long ago had said would happen." Jesus

---

In verses 50-54, Peter used a knife to cut a man that was arresting Jesus, but Jesus healed the man and told Peter to put back his knife—because God's kingdom is not built by violence against men but by obedience to God. How are you helping to build God's kingdom?

watched as every one of his cowboys jumped on their horses and loped away in fear.

The Head Honcho of the Church Questions Jesus

[57] The posse took Jesus and stood him before Caiaphas, the church's head honcho, and many other big wigs. [58] Pete had been followin' along like a Comanche warrior, at a distance and without bein' seen. He snuck in to the meetin' and sat down in the back to see what the outcome would be.

[59] This whole church institution was just lookin' for a way to lie about Jesus so they could sentence him to death. [60] After many attempts and people lyin' on the stand, they couldn't find a reason.

Then two fellows walked in and [61] said, "This cowboy said, 'I will destroy the church and rebuild it in three days.'"

[62] The head honcho stood up and asked Jesus, "Are you gonna answer these charges? What have you got to say about yourself?" [63] But Jesus kept his mouth closed.

The head honcho said, "I dare you to answer this one question, so help you God. Are you the Christ, the Boss' Son?"

[64] "Yup," Jesus said, "and I'm tellin' y'all right now that in the future you will see me sittin' right beside the Boss and ridin' back on the clouds of heaven."

[65] The head honcho broke into a fit of rage and spit flew from his mouth as he said, "He has called himself God! Why do we need more witnesses? Everyone in here just heard him. What do y'all think we should do now?"

[66] "String him up!!" they yelled.

[67] Then all the people took turns spittin' on Jesus and hittin' him in the face. All the while they [68] said, "If you're the Son of God, tell us who is hittin' you!"

Pete Denies Riding with Jesus

[69] Now Pete was still there and a young girl came up to him and said, "I know you! You rode with Jesus didn't you?"

[70] Without skippin' a beat, Pete said, "I ain't got a clue what you're yackin' about, ma'am."

[71] Pete saddled up and as he rode out of the courtyard, another young lady recognized

him and told everyone standin' there, "Hey look! There's one of Jesus' cowboys that rode with him right there."

⁷² Pete shook his head and hollered, "Why does everyone keep sayin' that? I ain't never seen that man before in my life."

⁷³ When things had settled down, some folks that were standin' close to Pete said, "We know you rode with Jesus. We can tell by your accent!"

⁷⁴ Then Pete started cussin' himself and everyone else and said, "I ain't never rode with no man named Jesus!"

Immediately, off in the distance, a rooster crowed. ⁷⁵ Then Pete remembered the words Jesus had spoken to him, "When you hear the cock crow, you will have denied ridin' with me three times." Pete loped away and wept like a child.

Matthew 27

Early that morning, the religious institution had decided to put Jesus to death. ² They tied him up and handed him over to Pilate, the Roman governor.

Judas Kills Himself

³ When Judas heard they were gonna kill Jesus, his heart was crushed because he was the cause of it all. He went back to the church and gave them the thirty pieces of silver back. ⁴⁻⁵ "I have sinned," he said, "I have double-crossed an innocent man."

"That don't matter to us," they replied. "This innocent blood will be on your hands, not ours!"

⁶ The segundos in the church picked up the money and said, "We can't even use this for our church bank account because it's blood money." ⁷ So they used the money to buy a little plot of land to use as a cemetery for foreigners. ⁸ That place is still called the field of blood to this day. ⁹ Then, the words of the great cowboy Jeremiah came true: "They took the thirty pieces of silver, the price of his double-cross, ¹⁰ and used it to by the foreigners field."

Jesus on Trial before Pilate

[11] Meanwhile, Jesus stood before the governor of the territory and the governor asked him, "Are you the Jews' boss?"

"Yup," Jesus replied.

[12] When he was accused by the head honchos of the church, he didn't answer. [13] Then Pilate asked him, "Don't you hear what they are sayin' about you?" [14] But Jesus didn't answer. He didn't say one word about any of the charges. His silence baffled Pilate.

Pilate Signs the Death Warrant

[15] There was an old tradition during this time of the year, to release one prisoner that the crowd chose. [16] There was a ruthless bandito named Barabbas that was in jail at this time. [17] When the crowd gathered around, Pilate asked them, "Which one do you want me to release: Barabbas, or Jesus who is called the Boss' Son?" [18] He knew that it was out of jealousy that they had shoe-horned Jesus and turned him in.

[19] While Pilate was actin' as judge and executioner, his wife sent him a note that said, "Don't have anything to do with that innocent fellow! I have been plagued by awful dreams because of this."

[20] But the head honchos of the church lobbied the crowd and persuaded them to release the bandito and have Jesus strung up.

[21] "Pick your poison and tell me which one you will have turned loose," said the governor.

"Barabbas the Bandito!" they all cried in unison.

[22] "If you choose Barabbas, what do you want done with Jesus?" asked Pilate.

They all yelled, "Kill him!"

[23] "Why? What in the world has this man done to deserve this?" asked Pilate.

But they got all slobber-mouthed and yelled, "Crucify him!"

[24] When Pilate saw that there was fixin' to be a riot, he dipped his hands in a horse trough and washed them sayin', "This is y'alls doin', not mine. I'm innocent of this man's blood and I wash my hands of this whole ordeal."

In verses 15-26, Pilate gave the crowd a choice: release Barabbas the political leader (see Mark 15:7) or Jesus the spiritual leader—and the people chose Barabbas. Today, if people were given the choice between a political leader or Jesus, who do you think they would choose?

In verse 24, even though Pilate said he would not kill Jesus, he didn't stop others from killing Jesus, so he was still guilty for his part. Have there been times when you gave up on doing the right thing?

²⁵ The crowd yelled, "Let this killin' fall on our children's souls!"

²⁶ Pilate then ordered the release of the bandito Barabbas and had Jesus horse-whipped before he was to be nailed to the cross.

Jesus is Mocked and Insulted

²⁷ Pilate's men took Jesus and put about 200 armed guards around him. ²⁸ They stripped him out of his jeans and shirt and slung a purple horse blanket around him like a robe. ²⁹ Then they wove together a crown of mesquite thorns and shoved it on his head. They gave him a stick to hold like a king's scepter and they knelt down mockingly in front of him sayin', "All hail the boss of the Jews!" ³⁰ They jerked his stick from him and beat him with it as they spit all over him. ³¹ After their sport with him, they took the purple blanket off and dressed him back in his trail gear. Then they tied him up and led him away to be nailed to the cross.

Jesus is Strung up on the Cross

³² As they traveled to the place they would kill him, a fellow named Simon was forced to carry the cross beam Jesus was tryin' to carry. ³³ They came to the place called Golgatha (which means Skull Hill). ³⁴ They offered Jesus a drink of wine mixed with a narcotic, but he spit it out as soon as he tasted it. ³⁵ When they had strung him up on the cross and nailed him to it to be sure he wouldn't fall off, they rolled dice to see who would get his gear. ³⁶ They all hunkered down to watch him die. ³⁷ Above Jesus' head, they nailed a crudely painted sign that said, "This here's Jesus, the Boss of the Jews." ³⁸ Two bank robbers were strung up beside him, one on his off-side and the other on his left. ³⁹ A bunch of no-accounts rode by and cussed Jesus ⁴⁰ sayin', "You claimed you were gonna destroy the church and rebuild it in three days! If you're the Boss' Son, come down off that cross and prove it, you coward!"

⁴¹ The head honchos of the church acted in the same sorry fashion. They made fun of him and said, ⁴² "He rescued other cowboys, now let's see if he can come down off that cross and rescue himself. If he does, then we'll believe he is who he says he is. ⁴³ He trusts in God. Let the Almighty save him if he really wants him. Jesus said himself, 'I am the Boss' Son.'" ⁴⁴ The bank robbers also talked real bad to him.

Jesus Dies

⁴⁵ From about noon until three, darkness covered the territory. ⁴⁶ About three o'clock

---

In verses 27-31, Jesus was mocked when the soldiers put a crown of thorns on his head, put a staff in his hand and bowed before him—before beating him with the staff. If you have been mocked for believing in Jesus, wouldn't you agree that Jesus himself was mocked far worse?

Jesus yelled out, "Eloi, Eloi, lama sabachthani?" —which translated into cowboy terms means, "My God, my God, why have you shucked out on me?"

⁴⁷ Some of the fellows standin' nearby said, "He's a hollerin' for Elijah!"

⁴⁸ One of the bystanders ran and filled his hat with soured wine and lifted it up to Jesus so he could get a drink. ⁴⁹ The rest of them said, "Leave him be. Let's see if Elijah will come a ridin' down to get him!"

⁵⁰ Then Jesus gave one last mighty yell and he died.

⁵¹ At that very moment, the drapery in the church that separated man from God was split down the middle startin' at the top and comin' down. The whole earth shook and boulders split wide open like busted watermelons. ⁵² Graves were opened up and a bunch of cowboys that had rode for the brand got up and walked, raised back to life. ⁵³ They rode out of the graveyards, and after Jesus came back to life, they went into Jerusalem and were seen by a lot of folks.

⁵⁴ When the deputy and those that were with him guardin' Jesus saw everything that was happenin', they were terrified and they cried out, "Oh no! He really was the Boss' Son."

⁵⁵ There was a bunch of women watchin' from afar. They had followed Jesus and cooked for him on many occasions. ⁵⁶ Among them were Mary Magdalene, James and Joses' momma Mary, and the mother of Zebedee's boys.

Jesus is Buried in a Cave

⁵⁷ When evenin' was a comin', a rich fellow named Joseph that had done some studyin' and travelin' with Jesus, ⁵⁸ went to Pilate and asked for Jesus' body. Pilate agreed and gave the order. ⁵⁹ Old Joseph took the body and wrapped it in a clean white sheet and ⁶⁰ put the body in a cave that had been hollowed out of a rock for Joseph when he died. They rolled a boulder in front of the entrance to keep the two legged and four legged coyotes out. ⁶¹ Mary Magdalene and the other Mary were sittin' there watchin' from nearby.

Deputies Guard the Tomb

⁶² The next day, the head honchos of the church and the Religious Know-it-alls went to Pilate. ⁶³ "Your honor," they said, "whilst that fellow we killed was still alive, he had

---

In verse 50, Jesus died to pay the price for your sins—which is eternal death—so that you could receive eternal life instead. If Jesus loved you enough to give up his life, do you think you could love him enough to commit your life to him?

said that he would come back to life three days later. [64] We want you to post some deputies at his grave to keep Jesus' cowboys from stealin' the body and claimin' that he come back to life. Jesus deceived many good and honest folks while he was alive, but if they pull this off, it will be worse than the first trick."

[65] "Take a few deputies," Pilate said. "Do whatever you think you need to do to make the grave secure." [66] They went and stretched some rope across the entrance with some mud at each end so's they could tell if it had been messed with. They told the deputies to stand guard and not let anyone mess with the body or the grave.

Matthew 28

Jesus Rides Back into Town

After the Day of Rest, at sunrise of the first day of the week, the two Marys went to visit Jesus' grave.

[2] All of a sudden there was a violent earthquake. A winged rider from heaven had flown down and rolled the boulder out of the way so they could see inside. [3] This angel looked like he was made of livin' lightnin' and his trail gear was as white as snow. [4] The deputies saw him and got so dadgummed scared that they fell down like dead men.

[5] The winged rider said, "Y'all don't be scared. I know that y'alls are lookin' for Jesus who was strung up and killed on that cross. [6] But he ain't here! He has rode back from the dead just like he said he would. Y'all come take a look and see that I ain't pullin' your leg. [7] Once yer satisfied that he ain't here, run and tell his cowboys: 'He has rode back from the dead and has struck a long trot for Galilee. There is where you'll meet him.' I've said what I came to say."

The Ladies See Jesus

[8] So the two ladies ran away from the grave. They was afraid, but at the same time they were plum happy. They ran as fast as they could towards where the cowboys were camped. [9] Suddenly they came upon Jesus sittin' there and he said, "Howdy!" They screamed for joy and fell down at his boots and worshiped him. [10] Then Jesus told 'em, "Don't be scared. Go and tell the boys of my outfit to meet me in Galilee."

In verses 5-6, the angel at the empty tomb told the women not to fear—Jesus had proved himself Lord by defeating death and coming back to life. Because Jesus proved himself Lord, do you know you don't have to fear for your own hide, the evil of other men, or even death?

The Head Honchos of the Church Bribe the Deputies

[11] While the women were goin' to tell Jesus' cowboys about what happened, the deputies rode into town and told the head honchos of the church about the winged rider and everything else that had happened. [12] The head honchos met together and came up with a devious plan. They gave the deputies a bunch of money and said, [13] "Tell people that Jesus' cowboys came in the middle of the night and bushwhacked you and stole Jesus' body. [14] If this report makes it back to Pilate, he will be fine with it and you won't get in trouble." [15] So the deputies pocketed their small fortunes and did what they were told to do. This lie has been told all over the place and is still thought to be true today.

Jesus Gives the Great Cow-mission

[16] The eleven remaining cowboys of Jesus' outfit rode out to Galilee to the mountain Jesus had told 'em about. [17] When they saw him, they took a knee before him and worshiped him, but even then, some of them had doubts. [18] Then Jesus walked up to 'em and said, "I've been made Boss over heaven's Green Pastures and all the pastures of this world. [19] Go now and recruit riders for my brand from all over the world, baptize them in the name of the Father and of the Son and of the Holy Ghost, [20] teachin' them to ride the cowboy way I have taught y'all. And remember this, I am always with you, even to the very end of every trail."

In verses 11-15, the religious leaders said the disciples took the body of Jesus, and that he did not come back to life—a lie that many people still believe today. How would you help someone who believed that lie to understand that Jesus really was brought back to life?

In verses 18-20, Jesus told his followers to tell the world the good news about how he covered death and came back to life, to baptize them in the name of the Father, the Son and the Holy Spirit and to teach them to live in obedience to God. Who could you bring closer to Jesus?

How to Become a Christian Cowboy

There was a cowboy many years ago that thought he was a doin' the right thing. This man had a bunch of Jesus' day workers beat up. He was even there when the very first one was killed for believin' in Jesus. This fellow went by the name of Saul.

Later, Jesus (after he had gone to heaven) stopped him on a country road and got his attention real quick. He told Saul that he was wrong 'bout a lot of things and Jesus got him straightened out. Jesus even went so far as to change not only the man he was, but also what his name was.

Jesus gave him a new life and a new name.

Paul (formerly Saul) would go on to write much of the New Testament. He told anyone who would listen that gettin' to heaven was available to anyone who trusted in Jesus and gave their lives to him. Paul laid out this path to eternal life in the book of Romans. He didn't make anything up, he just repeated what Jesus and all of the prophets in the Old Testament had been sayin' for a long time.

If you want to live a life with purpose and meaning that will extend all the way to eternity, all you have to do is follow the "Roamin' Trail" to salvation.

This trail isn't about fancy ceremonies or initiation rituals. It's about how you feel deep inside your guts. Saddle up and take a ride with me now as we travel down the "Roamin' Trail".

1. Romans 3:23 – 'cause everybody sins and needs God's forgiveness

2. Romans 5:8 – But God proved how much he loves us by this: While we were still sinners, Christ died for us.

3. Romans 6:23 – Workin' for sin's outfit pays ya in death, but God offers ya eternal life thru Jesus.

4. Romans 10:9 – We all deserve hell for the things we have done. But if you confess with your mouth that Jesus is Lord, believe with your heart that God raised Jesus from the dead, and that He took your punishment for you, you will be snatched up before you hit the fires.

5. Romans 10:13 – "EVERY sorry son-of-a-gun who calls on the name of the Lord will be saved!!!!"

6. Romans 5:1 – So, since we've been made right with God because of our

71

faith, we also have peace with God thru knowin' his Son Jesus Christ.

7. Romans 8:1 – No one can condemn those who have Jesus as their boss.

8. Romans 8:38-39 – Nothing can separate us from the love of God. Not life or death, not angels or demons, not the tallest mountain or deepest canyon, not the past, not the present, not the future, not any power, not a single thing in all of creation. This isn't just a promise, it's the Gospel Truth.

If you're still unsure, let's boil this down a tad just to be sure we understand a few things. Without these things, there is no truth to what you believe.

* **Admitting who you are**: We are all no good at all.

* **Need to be saved**: We are guilty of sin. We do deserve punishment. We want to be better. The only one who can save us is Jesus.

* **Believe in Jesus**: Intellectual belief means nothing. I believe that Julius Caesar was once the emperor of Rome, but that didn't change my life. You gotta believe with all your heart and soul.

* **Have faith**: Faith is trustin' God no matter what the situation or circumstance. Faith in God ensures a home in heaven, not a smooth trot on earth.

If you are ready, you can accomplish all of this by one simple conversation with God. If you feel all this deep inside your soul, allow me to help you with what you might say to him.

> *God, I'm a sorry sinner that realizes I cannot save myself, so I need you. I should be punished for what I am and what I have done, but I know that you took all that punishment for me. For this, I am eternally grateful. I am now askin' forgiveness and I am handin' you, not just the reins, but the whole bridle of my life. I have absolutely no control now. It's all up to you. Thank you for everything from the bottom of my heart and soul. I know now that I will meet you in heaven.*

Congratulations!! You are now a Christian Cowboy. The next step is to share this wonderful news with the world. Don't be shy. Shout it from the top of the mountain.

If we don't meet in this life, I'll see you in greener pastures.

Kevin Weatherby

Jake Hershey

Simplified Cowboy Version

About the Authors

Kevin Weatherby is the author of the *Gospel of Matthew: SCV*. He is the founder of Save the Cowboy and Campfire Cowboy Ministries. These ministries work to bring the message of the Gospel to the cowboy of today. Kevin is also the author of the *Great Cow-mission*, which features stories on the Christian way of life for cowboys in the real world. Kevin and his family live in Kiowa, CO.

Kevin can be reached at 1-303-621-0133 or through www.SaveTheCowboy.com.

Save The Cowboy is also the publisher of *Proverbs: SCV* and *Romans: SCV.*

Stephen Skelton is the author of the *John Wayne Movie Bible Study*, the *Bonanza Bible Study*, and the *Mayberry Bible Study*, among others. His DVD-based Bible studies use classic movies and TV programs as modern parables. For the *Gospel of Matthew: SCV*, Stephen provided the notes and reflection questions which appear at the bottom of the pages. Stephen and his family live in Nashville, TN.

Stephen can be reached at 1-877-463-4688 or through www.EntMin.com.

Made in the USA
San Bernardino, CA
29 April 2017